Sky

1

Students' Book

Longman

**Brian Abbs
Ingrid Freebairn**

Contents

1 🎧 Listen and read

Amy: Hi! I'm Amy. Amy Scott.
What's your name?

Tina: My name's Tina.

Toby: I'm Toby. Amy's my sister.

Mark: Tina!

Toby: Who's he?

Tina: He's my brother, Mark.

Mr Vialli: Good morning!
My name's Frank Vialli.

Mrs Scott: Good morning, Mr Vialli.
I'm Penny Scott.
Welcome to Bristol!

Mr Vialli: Thank you.

Now listen and repeat.

Everyday phrases
- Hi!
- Welcome to [Bristol]!
- Thank you.

4

I'm Banjo. Hi!

Look and learn

I'm ...	=	I am ...
He's ...	=	He is ...
She's ...	=	She is ...
My name's	=	My name is ...
What's ... ?	=	What is ... ?
Who's ... ?	=	Who is ... ?

2 Speak

Say *hello*.

A: *Hello! What's your name?*
B: *My name's Lidia. What's your name?*
A: *I'm Marek.*
B: *Hi, Marek!*

3 Write

Complete with *Who*, *He* or *She*.

1 *Who's* she?
2 ... 's my sister.
3 ... 's he?
4 ... 's my brother.

4 Write and speak

a) Write sentences about the people below.

1 *He's Robbie Williams.*

b) Ask about the people.

1 A: *Who's he?*
   B: *He's Robbie Williams.*

5 New words: Titles

a) Listen and repeat.

• **Mr** Scott • **Mrs** Scott • **Mr** Vialli • **Mrs** Vialli • **Miss** Kent

b) Match.

1 A: *Who's she?*
   B: *She's Miss Kent.*

① ... Kent ② ... Vialli ③ ... Scott ④ ... Scott ⑤ ... Vialli

6 New words: Greetings

a) Listen and repeat.

07:30 — Good morning.
14:30 — Good afternoon.
21:00 — Good evening.

b) Say *Good morning/afternoon/evening* to the famous people in Exercise 4 and welcome them to your town.

A: *Good afternoon, Mr Williams. Welcome to [Warsaw].*
B: *Thank you, Marek.*

7 Rap

The Greetings Rap

Go to page 92 and listen and join in the rap.

① Robbie Williams
② Kylie Minogue
③ Eddie Murphy
④ Penelope Cruz
⑤ Serena Williams

 **This is my family.**

1 🔲 Read

Read about the Vialli family.

①

My name's Tina. This is my family. This is my mother. Her name's Ann. And this is my father. His name's Frank.

③

This is my brother. His name's Mark.

②

This is my little sister. Her name's Susanna. She's very pretty.

④

And this is our cat. Her name's Bella. She's very friendly.

Now listen and repeat.

2 🔲 New words: Family

Listen and repeat.

• mother (mum) • father (dad) • parents • brother
• sister • grandmother • grandfather • aunt
• uncle • cousin • daughter • son • wife • husband

3 Write

Write the family words in Tina's family tree.
Which five words are not in the tree?

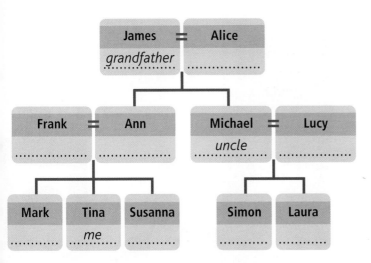

4 Act

You are one of the children in the family tree.
Introduce your family.

I'm Mark. This is my mother, Ann.

5 Game: Who am I?

You are one of the people in the family tree.
Others guess who you are.

A: *Michael is my father. Laura is my sister.*
B: *You're Simon!*

Look and learn

What's **his** name?
His name's Mark.

What's **her** name?
Her name's Tina.

6 Speak

Talk about the Vialli family. Look at Exercise 1.
A: *What's his name?*
B: *His name's Mr Vialli.*

7 Write

a) Complete the email with *my*, *his* or *her*.

Hi!
My name is Toby. This is my family.
This is ¹*my* mother, ²... name is Penny.
This is my father, ³... name is Steve.
This is me, ⁴... sister, Amy and
⁵... brother, Tim. And this is my dog.
⁶... name is Shep. He's very clever.
Bye!
Toby

b) Write an email to a new pen
friend with photos of your family.

8 Song

The Family Song

Go to page 92 and listen and complete the song.

③ Are you in Year 7?

1 🔊 Listen and read

Amy: Are you in Year 7, Tina?

Tina: Yes, I am.

Amy: How old are you?

Tina: I'm eleven.

Amy: Me too.

Toby: Hi, Tina.

Tina: Hello, Toby. Are you in Year 7 too?

Toby: No, I'm not. I'm in Year 8. I'm twelve.

Amy: Ssh! Here's Miss Kent. She's our teacher.

Toby: See you later.

Tina: OK. Bye.

Now listen and repeat.

Everyday phrases
- Yes/No.
- Me too.
- Ssh!
- Here's [Miss Kent].
- OK.
- See you later.
- Bye.

2 🔊 Numbers 1–50

Go to page 95 and listen and repeat the numbers.

3 🔊 Listen and write

a) Listen and write the missing numbers.

a) 3 + *8*   b) 9 + ...   c) ... + 2   d) ... + 10

e) 7 + ...   f) ... + 30   g) ... + 6

b) Now write the answers. Then listen and check.

a) 3 + 8 = 11

Look and learn

Are you in Year 7? Yes, **I am**./No, **I'm not**.

4 Game

Choose a character. The others must guess who you are.

A: *Are you Velma?*   A: *Are you Shaggy?*

B: *No, I'm not.*   B: *Yes, I am.*

(2) Shaggy   (3) Fred   (1) Velma   (4) Daphne   (5) Scooby

Look and learn

How old are **you**? **I'm** ten (years old).

How old is **he**? **He's** eleven.

How old is **she**? **She's** twelve.

5 Speak

a) Ask your friend.

A: *How old are you?*

B: *I'm ... . Are you ... too?*

A: *Yes, I am./No, I'm not. I'm ...*

b) Ask about the Vialli family.

A: *How old is Mark?*

B: *He's thirteen.*

I'm 43.   I'm 37.   I'm 11.   I'm 13.   I'm 6.

c) Now talk about your family.

6 Write

Complete with *am, 'm not, is, 's* or *are*.

1 How old ¹*is* Tina?   She ²... eleven.

2 How old ³... you?

3 ⁴... you in my class? Yes, I ⁵... .

4 ⁶... you twelve? No, I ⁷... ... .

5 Here ⁸... Miss Kent.

7 🔊 Rap

The Number Jive

Go to page 92 and listen and complete the rap.

This is my family. My mother, my father, my two sisters and my two brothers.

Hi!

Welcome to Willow Cottage.

Thank you, Mrs Green.

Are you hungry?

Yes, I am.

Me too.

Goodbye! See you tomorrow!

Who is this boy in the woods?

His name's Oliver and he's eleven years old.

His mother is very friendly.

OK. Where is Willow Cottage?

Oliver! Where are you?

The cottage isn't here and Oliver isn't here.

Very strange!

New words
- boy   • woods   • This way.
- Come with me.   • cottage
- hungry   • tomorrow
- where   • here   • strange

1 🎧 Listen and read

2 Check

Right (✓) or wrong (✗)?

1 Kelly and Jack are brother and sister. ✓
2 Jack is thirteen. ☐
3 Oliver is thirteen, too. ☐
4 Mrs Green is his sister. ☐
5 His mother is friendly. ☐

3 Act

Learn the story and act it out.

Revision

What's your name?

1 Complete the greetings and names.

① 09.30
② 14.30
③ 08.30
④ 19.30

1 *Good morning, Mr* Vialli.
3 ... , ... Scott.
2 ... , ... Kent.
4 ... , ... Scott.

2 Write the opposite words.

1 brother   *sister*
2 ...   mother
3 ...   aunt
4 grandfather   ...
5 husband   ...
6 ...   daughter

3 You are Toby. Introduce your family.

① Penny
② Steve

③ Amy
④ Tim

⑤ Susan
⑥ Andrew

1 *This is my mother. Her name's Penny.*

4 Choose the right words.

1 A: Hello. *What*'s your name?   ☐ Who   ☑ What
   B: Tina.
2 A: This is my brother.   ☐ his   ☐ her
   B: What's ... name?
3 A: Are you clever?   ☐ I'm   ☐ I am.
   B: Yes, ...
4 A: How old ... you?   ☐ are   ☐ is
   B: I'm ten.
5 A: Are you eleven?   ☐ I not ☐ I'm not
   B: No, ...
6 A: How old is your sister?   ☐ He's ☐ She's
   B: ... eleven.

5 Write the missing numbers.

1 one three five *seven* nine
2 two four six ... ten
3 nineteen eighteen seventeen ... fifteen
4 ten twenty thirty ... fifty
5 five ten fifteen twenty ...

6 Complete the dialogue.

• I'm • old • My • not • is • Are • your

Tim: Hello! I'm Tim. What's
        ¹*your* name?
Mark: ²... name's Mark. How
        ³... are you, Tim?
Tim: ⁴... seven. My brother,
        Toby ⁵... twelve.
        ⁶... you twelve too?
Mark: No, I'm ⁷... . I'm
        thirteen.

7 🔊 Sounds fun / iː / and / ɪ /

a) Listen and repeat.

She's Tina and he's Peter.
This is Jim and his sister, Greta.

b) Listen again and underline the / iː / sounds in red and the / ɪ / sounds in green.

8 🔊 Chatterbox

Complete the conversation. Listen and practise with Mark. Then practise with a friend.

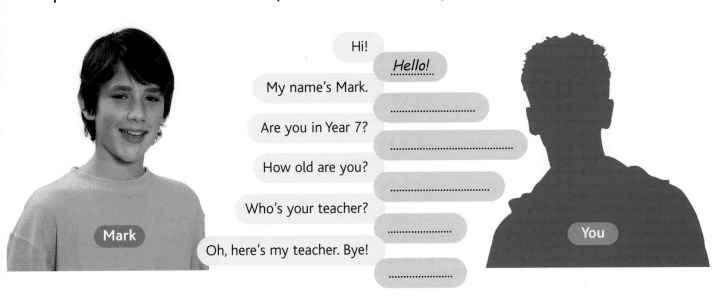

Mark

Hi!

My name's Mark.

Are you in Year 7?

How old are you?

Who's your teacher?

Oh, here's my teacher. Bye!

Hello!

....

....

....

....

....

You

9 Game: Find the match!

Play in pairs. Before you start, write the numbers 1–10 on cards and put them in a bag.

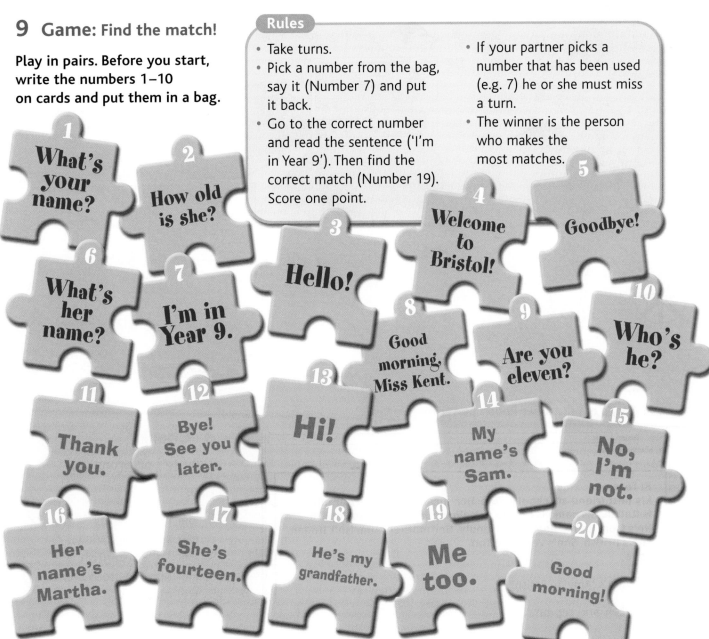

1 What's your name?

2 How old is she?

3 Hello!

4 Welcome to Bristol!

5 Goodbye!

6 What's her name?

7 I'm in Year 9.

8 Good morning, Miss Kent.

9 Are you eleven?

10 Who's he?

11 Thank you.

12 Bye! See you later.

13 Hi!

14 My name's Sam.

15 No, I'm not.

16 Her name's Martha.

17 She's fourteen.

18 He's my grandfather.

19 Me too.

20 Good morning!

Her father is Italian.

I'm from the UK.

1 New words: Countries and nationalities

a) Listen and repeat.

- Argentina – Argentinian
- Brazil – Brazilian
- China – Chinese
- France – French
- Germany – German
- Greece – Greek
- Italy – Italian
- Poland – Polish
- Portugal – Portuguese
- Russia – Russian
- Spain – Spanish
- Turkey – Turkish
- the UK (Great Britain) – British
- the USA (America) – American

b) Match the numbers on the map with the countries.

1 Number one is the USA.

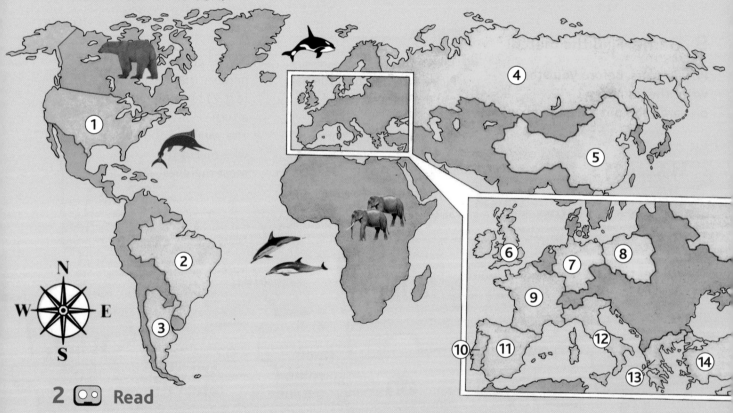

2 Read

Read Amy's email to her Polish pen friend, Teresa.

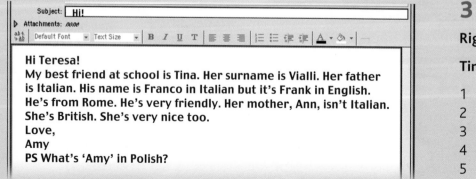

Subject: Hi!
Attachments: none

Hi Teresa!
My best friend at school is Tina. Her surname is Vialli. Her father is Italian. His name is Franco in Italian but it's Frank in English. He's from Rome. He's very friendly. Her mother, Ann, isn't Italian. She's British. She's very nice too.
Love,
Amy
PS What's 'Amy' in Polish?

Now listen and repeat.

3 Check

Right (✓) or wrong (✗)?

Tina:

1 Her friend is Amy Scott. ✓
2 Her surname is Vialli. ☐
3 Her father is British. ☐
4 Her father is from Rome. ☐
5 Her mother is Italian. ☐

14

Look and learn

Where **are you** from?	**I'm** from the UK.
Where **is he/she** from?	**He/She's** from Spain.
Where **are you** from?	**We're** from Poland.
Where **are they** from?	**They're** from Italy.

4 Speak

Ask and say where you are from.

A: *Where are you from, Consuela?*
B: *I'm from Spain. I'm Spanish.*

5 Write and speak

a) Write about the people.

1 *Barbara's from Poland. She's Polish.*
2 *Polly and Robert are from the UK.*
  They're British.

b) Ask and say where the people are from.

1 A: *Where is Barbara from?*
  B: *She's from Poland. She's Polish.*

① Hello! I'm Barbara. I'm from Poland.

② Hello! We're Polly and Robert. We're from the UK.

③ Hi, guys! We're Mike and Sue. We're from the USA.

④ Hi! I'm Hakan. I'm from Turkey.

⑤ Hello! I'm Sofia. I'm from Greece.

⑥ Hello! We're Matteo and Francesca. We're from Italy.

6 🔊 Listen and read

Teacher: Vialli's an interesting surname. Is your dad Italian?
Tina: Yes, he is.
Teacher: Is your mum Italian too?
Tina: No, she isn't. She's British.

Now listen and repeat.

Look and learn

Is he/she Italian?	Yes, **he/she is**.
Is he/she British?	No, **he/she isn't**.
Are they Italian?	Yes, **they are**.
Are they British?	No, **they aren't**.

7 Speak

Ask and answer about the people in Exercise 5.

1 A: *Is Barbara American?*
  B: *No, she isn't. She's Polish.*
2 A: *Are Polly and Robert Turkish?*
  B: *No, they aren't. They're British.*

1 Barbara/American?
2 Polly and Robert/Turkish?
3 Mike and Sue/Italian?
4 Hakan/Polish?
5 Sofia/Russian?
6 Matteo and Francesca/Spanish

8 Write

Complete with 'm, are, 's, is, isn't or aren't.

1 ¹ I'm from London. Where ² ... you from?
2 ³ ... you Italian?
  No, I ⁴ ... not.
3 ⁵ ... he American?
  Yes, he ⁶ ... .
4 ⁷ ... your friends British?
  No, they ⁸ ... .
5 No, Miss Rodriguez ⁹ ... British. She ¹⁰ ... from Spain.

9 Write

Write an email to a pen friend about your best friend at school. Look at Exercise 2.

My best friend at school is ... . His surname is ... .

15

7 It's an egg.

1 🎧 Listen and read

Tim: Toby! This is a good trick. Look! What's this?

Toby: It's an egg.

Tim: And what's that on the table?

Toby: It's a box.

Tim: That's right. Now, where's the egg? Is it in the box?

Toby: Yes, it is.

Tim: OK. Now, look. It isn't in the box.

Toby: Where is it? Is it under the table?

Tim: No, it isn't. It's here. Catch!

Toby: Yuk! The egg's bad. It's a silly trick!

Now listen and repeat.

Everyday phrases
That's right. Now, ...
Catch! Yuk!

2 🎧 New words

Listen and repeat.

① table ② orange ③ book ④ desk

⑤ ice cream ⑥ mobile phone ⑦ chair ⑧ egg ⑨ apple ⑩ bag

Look and learn

It's **a** box.   It's **an** egg.

It's = It is

3 Speak and write

a) Ask and answer about the pictures in Exercise 2.

A: *What's number one?*
B: *It's a table.*
A: *That's right.*

b) Write *a* or *an* before the words in Exercise 2.

1 a table   2 an orange

Look and learn

What's **this**?
It's a book.

What's **that**?
It's a table.

4 Act

You are Tim. Ask about the things in the hats.

1–5	6–10
A: *What's this?*	A: *What's that?*
B: *It's a table.*	B: *It's an orange.*

Look and learn

Where's the mobile phone?

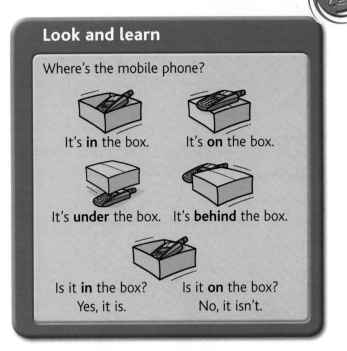

It's **in** the box.   It's **on** the box.

It's **under** the box.   It's **behind** the box.

Is it **in** the box?   Is it **on** the box?
Yes, it is.   No, it isn't.

5 Speak and write

a) Say where the mobile phone is.

1 A: *Where's the mobile phone?*
  B: *Look! It's under the desk.*

b) Write sentences.

The mobile phone is under the desk.

6 🔊 Listen

Listen and say where the phone is.

a) under the table ☐
b) in the bag ☐
c) on the chair ☐

7 🔊 Song

The Mermaid Song

Go to page 92 and listen and complete the song.

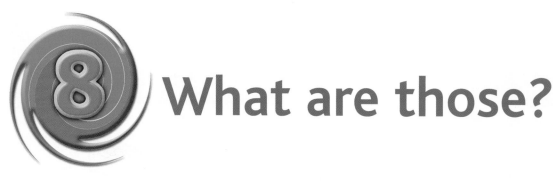

8 What are those?

1 📼 New words: Fruit

a) Listen and repeat.

• mango • pineapple • banana • pear • peach • grape
• lemon • cherry • strawberry • melon • plum • lime

b) Match.

Number one is a mango.

2 📼 Listen and read

Tim: What are those?
     Are they pears?

Woman: No, they're mangoes.
       They're from South America.
       They're very sweet.

Tim: Look, Amy! These are funny.
     Are they lemons?

Amy: I don't know. Excuse me, what
     are these?

Woman: They're limes. Have a taste.

Amy: Thanks. Ooh! It's sour!

Now listen and repeat.

> **Everyday phrases**
> • I don't know. • Have [a taste]. • Ooh!
> • Excuse me. • Thanks.

Look and learn

one pear	two pear**s**
one pineapple	two pineapple**s**
one peach	two peach**es**
one cherry	two cherr**ies**
one mango	two mango**es**

3 🔊 Write and speak

a) Write the plurals of the words in Exercise 1.

1 mangoes

b) Now listen and repeat the plurals.

Look and learn

What are **these**?
They're pineapples.

What are **those**?
They're mangoes.

They're = They are

4 Speak

Ask about the fruit, using *these* and *those*.

A: *What are these?*
B: *They're pineapples.*

A: *What are those?*
B: *They're mangoes.*

5 🔊 New words: Colours

a) Go to page 95 and listen and repeat the colours.

b) Look at the caps and say the colours.

1 *red*

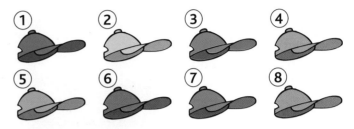

6 Speak

Ask about the colours of fruit.

A: *What colour is a banana?*
B: *It's yellow.*
A: *What colour are grapes?*
B: *They're purple or green.*

7 Read and write

Complete the advert with the names of the fruit.

THE Fruit MARKET

Buy your fruit at The Fruit Market.

The fruit is from all over the world.

English [1] *strawberries*, French [2] p… , Spanish [3] c… , South American [4] m… , [5] b… from the Caribbean and sweet purple [6] g… from Italy.

Come to *Fruit* for the best fruit in town!

8 🔊 Rap

The Fruit Rap

Go to page 92 and listen and complete the rap.

Countries and capitals

1 🔘 **Read**

Listen and read about Lee, Kelly and James.

My name's Lee Evans. I'm eleven. I'm American and I'm from New York. New York isn't the capital of the USA but it's a very big city. Washington DC is the capital. This is a photo of me in Washington DC.

I'm Kelly Packer. I'm Australian. I'm twelve years old and I'm from Canberra. Canberra is the capital of Australia but my favourite city in Australia is Sydney. It's a very beautiful city. This is a photo of me and my sister in Sydney.

Hello. I'm James Wagli. I'm British and I'm thirteen. I'm from Newcastle. It's a big city in the north of England. My grandmother and grandfather are from Bombay in India. This is a photo of me and three school friends on a school trip to London. London is the capital of the UK.

New words
- capital · big · city · photo · Australia(n)
- favourite · beautiful · India · school trip

2 Check

Read about Lee, Kelly and James again.
Complete the details.

	Lee	Kelly	James
First name:	Lee	Kelly	James
Surname:	...	...	...
Age:	...	...	...
Nationality:	...	...	...
Home town:	...	...	...
Capital city:	...	...	...

3 🔈 Listen

A student is on a school trip to London.
Listen and write down her details.

First name:	...
Age:	...
Nationality:	...
Home town:	Lyon
Capital city:	...

4 Speak

You are a famous person. Say your age, your
nationality, the name of your capital city and
your surname. Others guess who you are.

A: *I'm 40. I'm American. The capital of my country*
is Washington. My surname is Pitt.
B: *You're Brad Pitt!*

Project

Portfolio

Where I'm from

Writing tip

Capital letters (1)

We use capital letters for:
- the first letter in a sentence
  My name's ...
- names of people and places
  Lee Evans, New York ...
- nationalities
  American, ...
- the pronoun 'I'
  I'm eleven, ...

Read about the people in
Exercise 1 again and find
examples of capital letters.

Write

Write about where you live and your capital city.

My name is Carla. I'm Canadian. I'm twelve years old. I'm from Toronto in the south-east of Canada. Toronto isn't the capital of Canada but it's a big city. The capital of Canada is Ottawa.

10 Revision

1 What's the name of the country?

① nispa ② upalgort ③ dolanp

④ susria ⑤ taliy ⑥ recege

⑦ kuyter ⑧ gratenain ⑨ razibl

1 Spain

2 Group the nationality words under the right endings.

1 Americ-	2 Argentin-	3 Span-	4 Portugu-
5 Brit-	6 Fren-	7 Germ-	8 Brazil-
9 Chin-	10 Turk-	11 Gree-	12 Ital-

-ish	-(i)an	-ese	-k	-ch
	American			

3 Find 10 words in the word snake. Put *a* or *an* in front of them.

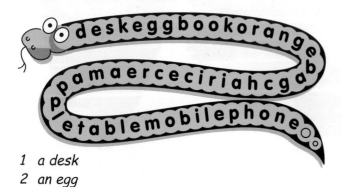

1 a desk
2 an egg

4 Choose the right words.

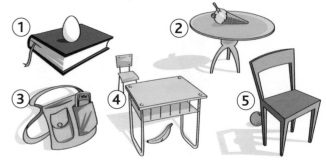

1 The egg is on/in the book.
2 The ice cream is on/under the table.
3 The mobile phone is in/on the bag.
4 The banana is on/under the desk.
5 The orange is behind/on the chair.

5 a) Complete the questions and answers.

Plate 1

1 What*'s this*?   It's *an apple.*
2 What *are these*?   They're *bananas.*
3 What ...   They're ...
4 What ...   It's ...
5 What ...   They're ...

Plate 2

6 What*'s that*?   It's *a plum.*
7 What *are those*?   They're *oranges.*
8 What ...   They're ...
9 What ...   They're ...
10 What ...   It's ...

b) Say what colour the fruit is.

1 *The apple is green.*
2 *The bananas are yellow.*

6 Complete the gaps in the conversation.

- • 'm • am • Are • are • 're
- • 's • Is • aren't • is • Are

Girl: ¹*Are* you British?

Boy: Yes, I ²... .

Girl: Where ³... you from?

Boy: I ⁴... from Manchester in England.

Girl: ⁵... your friends English too?

Boy: No, they ⁶... . They ⁷... Irish.

Girl: ⁸... your teacher here?

Boy: Yes, she ⁹... . She ¹⁰... over there.

7 🔲 Sounds fun / θ / and / ð /

a) Listen and repeat.
Thirty red strawberries
And thirteen juicy plums.
These are for my father
And those are for my mum.

b) Listen again and underline the / θ / sounds in red and the / ð / sounds in green.

8 🔲 Chatterbox

Complete the conversation. Listen and practise with Tina. Then practise with a friend.

Excuse me. Are you British?

No, I'm not.

Where are you from?

....

What's your surname?

....

That's an interesting name. How do you spell it?

....

Thanks. Where's your English teacher?

....

Oh, OK. See you later!

....

Tina

You

9 Game: Secret code

Look at the secret code!

| I J ! | J ' N | H B D L . |
| HI ! | I ' M | J A C K . |

| X I B U ' T | Z P V S | C F T U | G S J F O E ' T | O B N F ? |
| W H A T ' S | Y O U R | B E S T | F R I E N D ' S | N A M E ? |

Use the code to write a question.

| I J T | T V S O B N F | J T | C F D L I B N . |
| | | | |

| X I B U ' T | I J T | G J S T U | O B N F ? |
| | | | |

Now write the answer to the question.

23

We're in the kitchen.

1 🔘 Listen and read

Mark: Hi, Toby.

Toby: Oh hello, Mark. Come in. We're in the kitchen.

Amy: Hi, Mark. Look! This is a photo of our American friends.

Mark: What are their names?

Toby: Matt and Lisa. That's their house in the USA.

Mark: Wow! It's big. Is that their car in the garage?

Toby: Yes. It's American. It's a Ford.

Mark: Cool!

Now listen and repeat.

> **Everyday phrases**
> • Come in. • Look!
> • Wow! • Cool!

2 Check

Right (✔) or wrong (✗)?

1 Amy is in the kitchen. ☐
2 Matt and Lisa are from London. ☐
3 The car is Italian. ☐

3 🔘 New words: The house

a) Listen and repeat.

• dining room • sitting room
• kitchen • bathroom • toilet
• bedroom • hall • stairs
• garage • garden

b) Match.

1 garage

Look and learn

the kitchen   **the** bathroom
(one kitchen and one bathroom
in the house)

a table   **a** chair
(two or three chairs and tables
in the house)

Dido is on **a** chair in **the** kitchen.

Look and learn

We're Amy and Toby.
Our names are Amy and Toby.

They're Matt and Lisa.
Their names are Matt and Lisa.

4 Write

Complete the sentences with a, *an*, or *the*.

1 Shep is under _a_ chair in ... sitting room.
2 Is Suzy in ... dining room?
3 A: Where is ... dog?
   B: He's in the garden.
4 A: Is she in ... kitchen?
   B: No, she isn't. She's in ... garden with ... friend.
5 Is that ... apple on ... table?
6 Mum, is ... car in ... garage?
7 This is ... photo of our dog.

5 Speak

Say where you and your friend are in the house.

1 kitchen ✗   bathroom ✓
2 sitting room ✗   dining room ✓
3 toilet ✗   bedroom ✓
4 garden ✗   garage ✓

We aren't in the kitchen. We're in the bathroom.

6 Listen

Listen and write where the people and animals are.

1 Tim and Shep are in the ... .
2 Toby and Mark are in the ... .
3 Amy, Tina and Dido are in the ... .

7 Act

a) Say who you are and act the scenes.

1 A: *Who are you?*
   B: *We're Matt and Lisa Reed. This is our car.*
   A: *Wow! It's big!*

1 Matt and Lisa Reed: car

2 Prince William and Prince Harry: palace

3 Shrek, Donkey and Princess Fiona: garden

4 David and Victoria Beckham: house

b) Talk about the people.

1 A: *Who are they?*
   B: *They're Matt and Lisa Reed. That's their car.*
   A: *Wow! It's big!*

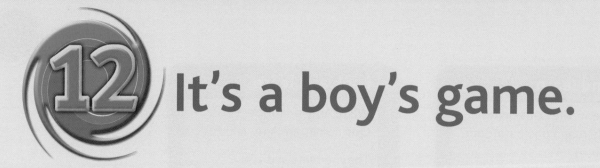

12 It's a boy's game.

1 🔊 Listen and read

Amy: I'm bored.

Toby: What about a game of cricket?

Amy: Cricket's a boy's game.

Tina: No, it isn't, Amy. It's fun.

Mark: OK. Boys against girls.

Toby: All right. Here's my cricket bat and a ball.

Amy: That's Tim's ball.

Toby: Never mind. OK. Mark, Dan and I are in the boys' team, and Amy, Tina and Linda are in the girls' team.

Amy: Come on. Bowl the ball.
Oh no! That's Mr Adam's window!

Tim: ... and that's my ball!

Now listen and repeat.

Everyday phrases
- I'm bored.   • What about [a game of cricket]?
- It's fun.   • All right.   • Never mind.
- Come on.   • Oh no!

2 Check

Right (✓) or wrong (✗)?

1 The boys and girls are in the garden. ☐
2 Tina is bored. ☐
3 Cricket is a game with three teams. ☐

3 New words: Common possessions

a) Listen and repeat.

- computer • computer game • camera • cricket bat • radio
- watch • bike • ball • skateboard • CD • Discman • stereo

b) Match.

1 watch

4 Listen

Listen to four scenes and write the missing word when you hear a BLEEP.

1 *bike* 2 ... 3 ... 4 ...

Look and learn

Tim**'s** ball   the boy**s'** team

5 Speak

Say if the things are Toby's or Amy's.

1 *It's Toby's camera.*

TS = Toby Scott AS = Amy Scott

6 Write

Complete the sentences with *the boys'* or *their parents'*.

1 It's *the boys'* computer game.
2 It's *their parents'* car.
3 They're ... bikes.
4 It's ... mobile phone.
5 They're ... skateboards.
6 It's ... stereo.

7 Game

Collect an object (e.g. a pen, book, rubber) from each student and put it in a bag. Take one out, and guess who owns it.

A: *Is it Tom's pen?*
B: *No, it isn't. It's Giulia's pen.*
C: *You're wrong. It's my pen.*

There isn't a garden.

1 **Read**

Our homes
Dan from the UK

I'm Dan. I'm a student at Clifton Park School in Bristol. This is my home. It's a houseboat on the river. In the sitting room there's a big red sofa, an armchair, a TV, a desk, a chair and a computer. In the kitchen there are some cupboards. In my bedroom there are two beds under the window for me and my brother. There's also a wardrobe. There are some posters of Manchester United on the door. It's fun to live on a houseboat. There isn't a garden but there are some plants, a table and some chairs on the deck. It's great in summer.

Dan Pastakia.
Bristol, UK.

Now listen and repeat.

2 **New words: House and furniture**

Listen and repeat.

 ① television/TV   ② bed   ③ window   ④ wardrobe   ⑤ armchair

 ⑥ sofa    ⑦ poster   ⑧ door   ⑨ plant   ⑩ lamp   ⑪ cupboard

3 Check

List the things in Dan's houseboat.

1 In the sitting room *sofa,*........................
2 In the bedroom ....
3 On the deck ....

Look and learn

a cupboard **some** cupboards
a book **some** books

4 Game

a) Look at the picture for one minute. Close your books. List the things.

1 *a sofa*
2 *some books*

b) Now open your books and check.

Look and learn

There's a TV.
There are some cupboards.
There's = There is

5 Speak and write

Say what is in the pictures in Exercise 4. Then write sentences.

1 *There's a sofa.*
2 *There are some books.*

Look and learn

Is there a TV?
  Yes, **there is**./No, **there isn't**.
Are there any cupboards?
  Yes, **there are**./No, **there aren't**.
There isn't a cupboard.
There aren't any plants.

6 Speak

Ask about your friend's flat or house. Ask about:

• a sitting room in the house
• plants in the house
• a TV in the kitchen
• cupboards in the parents' bedroom
• posters in your friend's bedroom
• a garden behind the house
• a garage under the house

A: *Is there a sitting room in your flat/house?*
B: *Yes, there is./No, there isn't.*
A: *Are there any plants in your flat/house?*
B: *Yes, there are. /No, there aren't.*

7 Listen

Listen to Tina talking about her bedroom. Tick the correct room.

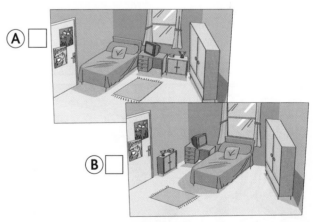

Ⓐ ☐
Ⓑ ☐

8 Draw and write

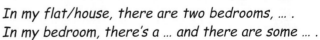Portfolio

Draw a plan of your flat or house and write about it. Use Exercise 1 to help you.

In my flat/house, there are two bedrooms, ...
In my bedroom, there's a ... and there are some ... .

9 Song

The Crazy House Song

Go to page 92 and listen and complete the song.

Take Five!

Annie | Cleo | Flame | Danny | Dex | Ray Madison

1

Hi! My name's Annie and these are my friends, Cleo, Flame, Danny and Dex. Cleo, Danny and I are British, Flame is Brazilian and Dex is American.

2

The name of our band is 'Take Five'! We're in the Pop Star Competition. We're in London with our parents in a big hotel. Tomorrow is the final of the competition.

3

Our hotel is great. In the girls' room there are three beds and a TV and in the boys' room there's a small kitchen.

New words

- band • pop star • competition
- hotel • tomorrow • final
- great • small • record • ready
- Listen! • winner • song

1 🎧 Listen and read

2 Check

Complete the missing words.

1 There are *three* girls and ... boys in *Take Five*.
2 Annie, Cleo and Danny are British, Flame is ... and Dex is ... .
3 In the girls' hotel room, there are three ... and a ... .
4 Ray Madison is from ... *Records*.
5 *Hey, Listen!* is the name of their ... .

3 Act

Learn the story and act it out.

31

Revision

1 Write the words in two groups.

• bike • sofa • television • ball • stereo • armchair • radio • wardrobe • skateboard • cupboard • cricket bat • computer

In the house	In the garden
sofa	bike

2 Complete the sentences with *my, your, his, her, our* and *their*.

1 A: Where's *my* pen?
  B: Is it in ... school bag?
2 This is my teacher. ... name's Miss Kent.
3 We're students in Year 7. ... names are Amy and Tina.
4 A: Is that your parents' car?
  B: No, ... car is black.
5 My brother is in ... room and ... sister is with ... friend.

3 Write the missing words.

Bobby Conrad is 📷 ¹*American.*

In his 🏠 ²... in Los Angeles, there are

🎲 ³... televisions. There's one in his

🛏 ⁴... room, and one in his parents'

room. There's a very big 📺 ⁵... in the

sitting room, one in the 🔧 ⁶... and a

very small one in the 🛁 ⁷... room!

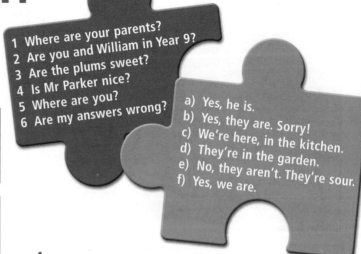

1 Where are your parents?
2 Are you and William in Year 9?
3 Are the plums sweet?
4 Is Mr Parker nice?
5 Where are you?
6 Are my answers wrong?

a) Yes, he is.
b) Yes, they are. Sorry!
c) We're here, in the kitchen.
d) They're in the garden.
e) No, they aren't. They're sour.
f) Yes, we are.

4 Match the questions and answers.

1 d

5 Write the apostrophes in the right places.

1 My sister's name is Emma.
2 Kim is a boys name and a girls name.
3 My friends names are Jason, Ben and Tom.
4 Theres a small computer in my parents room.
5 They arent in the kitchen, theyre in the sitting room.
6 A: Is that Tobys radio? B: No, its Marks.

6 Complete with *'s, is, are, isn't* or *aren't*.

1 There's a cricket bat in the garden.
2 There ... some strawberries in the garden.
3 ... there a phone in your kitchen?
4 There ... a stereo in my room but there ... a radio.
5 ... there any CDs in the sitting room?
6 There ... any boys in my class.

7 Score a goal with *some* or *any*!

1 Are there *any* books in the cupboard?
2 There are ... posters on my bedroom door.
3 Are there ... good songs on that CD?
4 There are ... bananas in the fruit bowl but there aren't ... cherries.

8 Chatterbox

Complete the conversation. Listen and practise with Amy. Then practise with a friend.

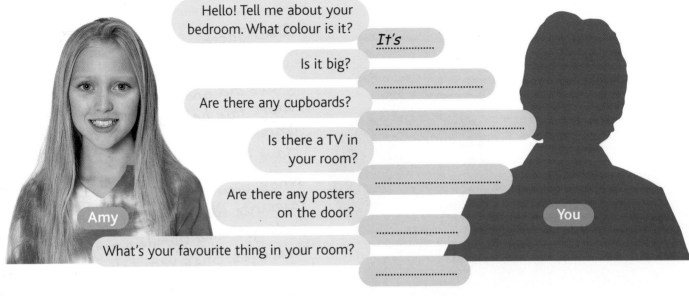

Hello! Tell me about your bedroom. What colour is it?

It's _____

Is it big?

....

Are there any cupboards?

....

Is there a TV in your room?

....

Are there any posters on the door?

....

What's your favourite thing in your room?

....

Amy

You

9 Sounds fun / ə /

a) Listen and repeat.

Here is Tina with her brother
And her father and her mother.
Where's her little sister?
She's using the computer.

b) Listen again and underline the / ə / sounds in red.

10 Game: Wordfinder

Find the right letters to spell some good presents.

Wordfinder

	1	2	3	4	5	6
A	J	M	L	A	X	Y
B	E	C	B	N	T	R
C	G	M	O	S	P	M
D	E	T	I	D	F	Q
E	V	U	G	K	A	W
F	Z	M	R	S	K	E

1 F3 A4 D4 D3 C3

1 R A ... ...

2 B2 A4 C6 D1 F3 E5

3 F4 E4 A4 B5 B1 B3 C3 A4 F3 D4

16 She's got blonde hair.

1 Read

Toby's class has got a Pen Friend Club. This is Toby's first letter to a new pen friend.

Dear Jacek,

My name is Toby Scott. I'm twelve years old and I'm from Bristol. I've got short fair hair and blue eyes. What colour hair and eyes have you got? Have you got short hair or long hair?

Who's your favourite film star? My favourite film star is Nicole Kidman. She's got long blonde wavy hair and blue eyes. She's very tall. I haven't got her autograph but I've got a poster. She's really cool. My sister's favourite film star is Richard Gere. He's old! He's got grey hair and brown eyes. Have you got any brothers or sisters? Please write soon.

Best wishes,

Toby

Now listen and repeat.

2 Check

Complete the information.

	Toby Scott	Nicole Kidman	Richard Gere
Hair	short fair		
Eyes	blue		

3 New words:

Hairstyles and colours

Listen and repeat.

① long ② short ③ medium length ④ curly ⑤ straight ⑥ wavy

⑦ spiky ⑧ blonde ⑨ brown ⑩ black ⑪ red ⑫ grey ⑬ dark ⑭ fair

Look and learn

I've got red and blue hair.

What colour hair **have** you **got**?
I've got brown hair.
Have you **got** short hair?
Yes, I **have**./No, I **haven't**.

I've got = I have got
I haven't got = I have not got

4 Game: Who am I?

You are a person in this book. Others ask questions and guess who you are.

A: *What colour hair have you got?*
B: *I've got blonde hair.*
A: *Have you got long hair or short hair?*
B: *I've got long hair.*
A: *I know. You're Amy!*

5 Write

Write a sentence about yourself.

I've got wavy brown hair and green eyes.

Look and learn

What colour hair **has** she/he **got**?
She's/He's got black hair.
Has she/he **got** long hair?
Yes, she/he **has**./No, she/he **hasn't**.

She's/He's got = She/He has got
She/He hasn't got = She/He has not got

6 Speak and write

a) Ask and answer about the people.

1 Catherine Zeta-Jones
A: *What colour hair has she got?*
B: *She's got black hair.*
A: *Has she got long hair or short hair?*
B: *She's got long hair.*

b) Write about the people.

1 *Catherine Zeta-Jones has got long black hair and brown eyes.*

7 Write and speak

a) Complete with *have*, *haven't* or *has*.

A: *Have you got any brothers or sisters?*
B: *No, I … . / Yes, I … . I've got a sister.*
A: *What colour hair … she got?*
B: *She's got brown hair.*

b) Ask and talk about your family.

8 Listen

Complete the information about Dan's brother.

Name:	Age:
Hair:	Eyes:

9 Write

Write to a new pen friend. Describe yourself, your family and your favourite film star. Use Toby's letter in Exercise 1 to help you.

Portfolio

① Catherine Zeta-Jones
② Jim Carrey
③ Gillian Anderson
④ Nicole Kidman
⑤ Richard Gere
⑥ Will Smith

17 How many animals have you got?

1 🔈 New words: Animals

a) Listen and repeat.

• horse • cow • sheep • goat • chicken • duck • pony
• calf • lamb • goose • chick

b) Match.

Number one is a cow.

Note!

Irregular plurals

one sheep	two sheep
one calf	two calves
one goose	two geese

4 Check

List the animals on the farm.

1 some horses

5 🔈 Numbers 50–100

Go to page 95 and listen and repeat the numbers.

6 🔈 Game

Listen and write the next number when you hear the 'ping'.

a) *sixty* b) … c) … d) … e) …

2 🔈 Listen

Listen and write the six animals you hear.

1 It's a cow.

3 🔈 Listen and read

Julie: Hello, everyone! My name's Julie. Welcome to Oaktree Farm.

Toby: Julie, how many animals have you got here?

Julie: We've got about a hundred.

Amy: Have you got any ponies?

Julie: No, we haven't but we've got some horses, some cows, some sheep and some chickens. Come and look.

Tim: Amy! Have they got any dinosaurs?

Amy: No, they haven't. Don't be silly, Tim!

Tim: It's only a joke!

Now listen and repeat.

Everyday phrases
• Hello, everyone.
• About [a hundred].
• Come and look.
• Don't be silly!
• It's only a joke!

Look and learn

Have you got **any** chickens?
Yes, we have.

Have you got **any** ponies?
No, we haven't.

How many animals have you got?
We've got about a hundred.

We've got = We have got
We haven't got = We have not got

Look and learn

They've got **some** sheep but they haven't got **any** goats.

They've got = They have got
They haven't got = They have not got

8 Read and write

Read and complete with *have got*, *'ve got* or *haven't got*.

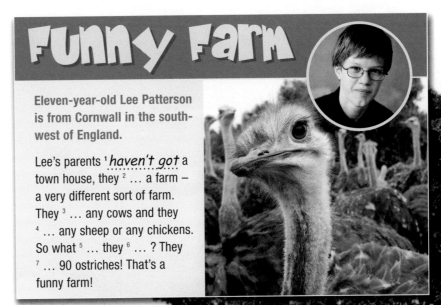

Funny Farm

Eleven-year-old Lee Patterson is from Cornwall in the south-west of England.

Lee's parents [1] *haven't got* a town house, they [2] … a farm – a very different sort of farm. They [3] … any cows and they [4] … any sheep or any chickens. So what [5] … they [6] … ? They [7] … 90 ostriches! That's a funny farm!

7 Act

One of you is Julie. Use the information to talk about your animals.

A: *Julie, have you got any chickens on the farm?*

B: *Yes, we have.*

A: *How many chickens have you got?*

B: *We've got about thirty. Come and look.*

Chickens	30	Cows	15
Goats	0	Horses	5
Ponies	0	Sheep	50

9 Rap

The Funny Farm Rap

Go to page 93 and listen and join in the rap.

18 It's five past four.

1 🎧 Listen and read

Toby: Hurry up! There's a film about tigers at four o'clock. What time is it?

Dan: It's five past four. We're late!

Toby: Excuse me, what time's the film?

Girl: There isn't a film today. Today's Tuesday. Sorry, boys.

Toby: Oh! When's the film about tigers?

Girl: It's on Thursday at four o'clock.

Dan: You're hopeless, Toby.

Girl: There's an interesting lecture about insects today.

Toby: Er ... no, thanks.

Now listen and repeat.

Everyday phrases
- Hurry up!
- We're late!
- Sorry, [boys].
- You're hopeless.
- No, thanks.

2 Check

Right (✓) or wrong (✗)?

a) They're late. ☐
b) The film is today. ☐
c) The film is about insects. ☐

3  The time

Listen and repeat.

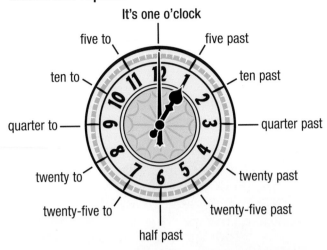

It's one o'clock

five to — five past

ten to — ten past

quarter to — quarter past

twenty to — twenty past

twenty-five to — twenty-five past

half past

Look and learn

What time is it?/What's the time?

It's four **o'clock**. It's five **past** four. It's ten **to** five.

4 Speak and write

a) Look at the clocks and speak.

A: *Hurry up!*
B: *Why? What time is it?*
A: *It's six o'clock. We're late!*

b) Now write the times.

1 It's six o'clock.

5  Listen

Listen and tick the right times.

1	a) 11.45 ☐		3	a) 15.30 ☐
	b) 12.15 ☐			b) 13.30 ☐
2	a) 6.50 ☐		4	a) 09.05 ☐
	b) 18.50 ☐			b) 08.55 ☐

6  New words: Days of the week

Go to page 95 and listen and repeat the days of the week.

Look and learn

When is the film?
It's **on** Thursday **at** four o'clock.

7 Speak

Ask and answer about the film times.

Films on TV next week		
Monday	17.00	Night and Day
Tuesday	18.20	American Girl
Wednesday	15.30	Weekend in Warsaw
Thursday	16.00	Dogs' Day
Friday	19.10	Two and Two are Five
Saturday	17.45	The Picture
Sunday	18.50	Wild Horses

A: *When's 'Night and Day'?*
B: *It's on Monday at five o'clock.*

8  Listen

Listen and complete the days and times of the programmes.

Day	Time	TV Programme
...	*5.00*	Blue Peter
...	...	The Simpsons
...	...	Friends

9 Read and write

a) Complete Amy's text message with *on* or *at*.

b) Write a text message to a friend about a visit to the cinema.

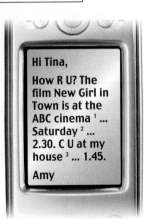

Hi Tina,

How R U? The film New Girl in Town is at the ABC cinema [1] ... Saturday [2] ... 2.30. C U at my house [3] ... 1.45.

Amy

10  Song

The Time Song

Go to page 93 and listen and complete the song.

19 Houses in the UK

1 🎧 **Read**

Listen and read about Damon, Natalie, Sangeeta and Ryan.

My home

Damon

I live with my parents and two brothers in a flat in Manchester. Our flat has got two bedrooms, a sitting room, a kitchen, a bathroom and a small balcony. We haven't got a garden but there's a park behind the flat.

Natalie

I live with my father, my mother and my sister in a cottage in South Wales. The cottage is old but it's nice. We've got two cats and a dog, and we've got a big garden with four apple trees!

Sangeeta

I live in Edinburgh. Our house is a detached house and it's quite big. My sister and I have got our own bedrooms. We've got a garden and a garage too. Our road is very quiet. It's too quiet sometimes!

Ryan

I live in a terraced house in Belfast. We haven't got a garage but we've got a small garden. We've got lots of neighbours and our street is quite noisy but it's fun.

 ① A detached house

 ② A terraced house

 ③ A cottage

 ④ A block of flats

New words

• live • flat (block of flats) • balcony • park
• cottage • apple tree • terraced • neighbours
• street • quite • noisy • fun • detached
• own • road • too quiet • sometimes

2 Check

a) Match the people with the homes.

Damon – Picture 4

b) Put a tick in one of the right columns.

Who has got:	Damon	Natalie	Sangeeta	Ryan
a house in Edinburgh? a cottage? a small garden? a balcony? lots of neighbours? three pets?			✓	

3 🔊 Listen

Listen and complete the facts.

Name:	*John*
Nationality:	....
Home:	*an apartment*
Where:	....
Number of bedrooms:	....
Number of people in his family:	....

4 Speak

You are one of the people in Exercise 1. Say two things about where you live. Don't say the type of house and don't say where it is. The others must guess who you are.

A: *We've got a garden. Our road is quiet.*
B: *You're Sangeeta!*

Project

Portfolio

Houses in my country

Write

Collect pictures of three different types of houses in your country. Write about the house in each picture.

• What is it?
• Where is it?
• What rooms has it got?
• Is there a garden or garage?

Writing tip

Full stops and commas

• Put a full stop at the end of a sentence and start the next word with a capital letter.

It's near Central Park. We've got two bedrooms.

• Join a list of more than two things with a comma, e.g.

Our flat has got two bedrooms, a sitting room, a kitchen, a bathroom and a small balcony.

Find more examples of full stops and commas in the texts in Exercise 1.

A house in my country
This is a villa in the south of Italy. Downstairs there's a sitting room, a kitchen and a toilet and upstairs there are three bedrooms and a bathroom. It's got a big garden and a swimming pool but it hasn't got a garage.

Revision

1 Complete the dialogues.

①
A: *Has* he *got* long hair?
B: No, *he hasn't*.
   He*'s got* short hair.

②
A: ... she ... straight hair?
B: No, ... She ... .

③
A: Have you ... dark hair?
B: No, ... I ... .

④
A: ... he ... green eyes?
B: No, ... He ... .

⑤
A: ... you ... blonde hair?
B: No, ... We ... .

⑥
A: ... they got wavy hair?
B: No, ... They ... .

2 Write the missing words.

Carlo Pino and his family are from New

Mexico in the ¹*USA*. Their ²...

is small. They haven't got a ³... or a

 ⁴... but they've got a ⁵... and

a ⁶... . Carlo's family has got some

animals too: five ⁷... and three

 ⁸... . They haven't got any 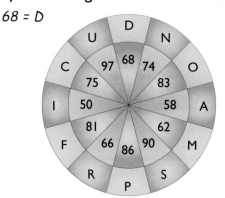 ⁹ ...

or any ¹⁰... .

3 Write the plurals.

1 chicken *chickens*   5 pony   ...
2 goose   *geese*   6 calf   ...
3 goat   ...   7 ostrich ...
4 horse   ...   8 sheep   ...

4 Number puzzle

a) Add 5 to each number, then write the new number.

63	45	69	78	85	53	92	61
68							

b) Find the right letter on the wheel.

68 = D

c) Write the letters to find out Tim's favourite animal.

D ... ...

5 Complete the days of the week.

M O N D A Y   F R ... D A Y
T U ... S D A Y   S ... T ... R D A Y
W E D ... E ... D A Y S ... ... D A Y
T ... U ... S D A Y

6 Write the times.

1 ten past six

① ② ③ ④ ⑤ ⑥

42

7 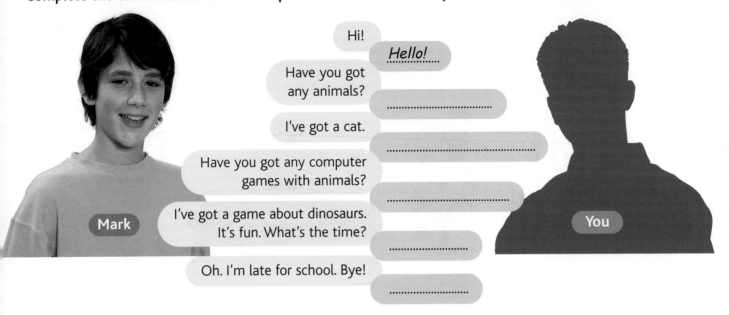 Chatterbox

Complete the conversation. Listen and practise with Mark. Then practise with a friend.

Mark: Hi!
You: *Hello!* ....

Mark: Have you got any animals?
You: ....

Mark: I've got a cat.
You: ....

Mark: Have you got any computer games with animals?
You: ....

Mark: I've got a game about dinosaurs. It's fun. What's the time?
You: ....

Mark: Oh. I'm late for school. Bye!
You: ....

8 Game: Guess who!

Listen and match the descriptions with the correct pictures.

1 is picture ...

A

B

C

D

E

F

9 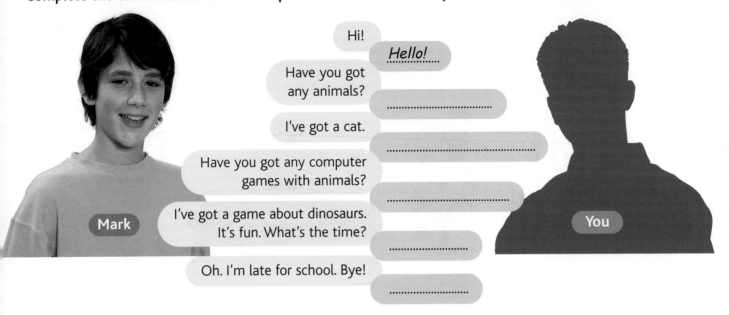 Sounds fun / h /

a) Listen and repeat.
Who's he? He's Harry Potter.
Harry Potter has got dark hair.
His school is Hogwarts.
He studies magic there.

b) Listen again and underline the / h / sounds in red.

1 🎧 **Read**

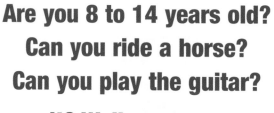

Blue Skies
Adventure Camp

Are you 8 to 14 years old?
Can you ride a horse?
Can you play the guitar?

You can't? Well, come and learn!

Blue Skies Adventure Camp is a holiday camp for children in the south-west of England. There are lots of exciting things to do at the camp.

Come to Blue Skies Adventure Camp and have some fun.
Telephone on 0870 555 1234 (24 hours).

Note!

Irregular plurals

child	children
man	men
woman	women

Now listen and repeat.

2 New words: Free time

a) Listen and repeat.

- swim under water • sing a song • use a computer
- read a map • make an omelette • play table tennis
- play the guitar • ride a horse • skateboard
- sail a boat • play chess • play the piano

b) Match with the pictures in Exercise 1.

1 sail a boat

3 Listen and read

Amy: Look at this poster, Tina. Can you ride a horse?

Tina: No, I can't. Can you?

Amy: Yes, I can, but I can't ride very well.

Now listen and repeat.

Look and learn

I/you/he/she/it/we/they

I can ride a horse.
I can't play the guitar.

I can't = I cannot

4 Speak

a) Say two things you can do and two things you can't do. Look at the list in Exercise 2.

I can swim under water and I can make an omelette. I can't ride a horse and I can't sail a boat.

b) Now write two sentences about you.

Look and learn

Can you ride a horse?
Yes, I can./No, I can't.

Can he/she ride a horse?
Yes, he/she can./No, he/she can't.

Can they ride a horse?
Yes, they can./No, they can't.

5 Speak and write

a) Ask a friend and note the answers. Use the words in Exercise 2.

A: *Can you ride a horse, Anna?*

B: *Yes, I can./No, I can't./Yes, I can, but I can't ride very well.*

b) Tell the class.

Anna can swim under water, but she can't ride a horse.

c) Write what both of you can and can't do.

We can use a computer, but we can't sail a boat.

6 Listen

Jason and Rod are at Blue Skies Camp. Listen and say what they can and can't do.

1 They can ... .
2 They can't ... .

7 Read and write

Read and complete Jason's letter to his parents.

Dear Mum and Dad,
    The adventure camp is great. I ¹... do lots of new things now. I ²... skateboard and ³... a boat. I can't ⁴... a map or ⁵... a horse very well, but that's OK. The teachers here ⁶... very nice and the children are friendly but the food's horrible! I ⁷... got a new friend. His name ⁸... Rod.
See you soon.
    Love
        Jason

8 Write

Imagine you are at the summer camp. Write a letter home.

45

Can I have an ice cream?

1 🎧 Listen and read

Girl: Hello. Can I help you?

Toby: Yes, please. How much are the ice creams?

Girl: They're £1.40.

Mark: What flavours have you got?

Girl: We've got strawberry, vanilla and chocolate.

Mark: Can I have a strawberry ice cream, please?

Toby: And can I have a chocolate ice cream?

Tina: Have you got any milkshakes?

Girl: Yes, they're £2.

Tina: OK. Can I have a banana milkshake, please?

Girl: Sure. That's £4.80, please.

Toby: Oh no! I've only got £4.60!

Tina: No, you haven't.
You've got £4.80.
You can't count.

Now listen and repeat.

Everyday phrases
- Can I help you?
- Yes, please.
- Sure.
- I've only got [£4.60].

2 Check

Read the dialogue again. Note who wants what.

	Name
a strawberry ice cream a chocolate ice cream a banana milkshake	

3 New words: Food and drink

a) Listen and repeat.

- chocolate/vanilla ice cream
- strawberry/banana milkshake
- cola • lemonade • orange juice
- mineral water • hot chocolate

b) Match.

1 orange juice

Which two words are not in the pictures?

Look and learn

Can I have a vanilla ice cream, please?
Yes, sure.

4 Speak

Say what you want.

A: *Can I have an orange juice, please?*
B: *Yes, sure.*

5 British money

Go to page 95 and listen and repeat the British money.

Look and learn

How much is a chocolate milkshake? It's £2.
How much is it? It's £2.

How much are the ice creams? They're £1.40.
How much are they? They're £1.40.

Menu

Ice creams
vanilla, chocolate, strawberry
£1.40

Milkshakes
chocolate, strawberry, banana
£2.00

Drinks
cola, lemonade, orange juice, mineral water, hot chocolate
£1.25

6 Speak

Ask about the prices of the things on the menu.

A: *How much is an ice cream?*
B: *It's £1.40.*

7 Write

Portfolio

Make a café menu.

8 Act

Work in groups. You are in a café. You've got £10. Act a conversation. One of you is a waiter. Use your menu from Exercise 7.

A: *Hello. Can I help you?*
B: *Yes, please. How much is a ... ?*
A: *It's ... .*
B: *Can I have ... ?*
A: *Yes, sure.*

9 Listen and write

a) You're in a café. Listen and write the order.

b) What is the total price? Listen again and see if you were right.

23 Don't point!

1 New words: The body

a) Listen and repeat.

- eye • head • nose • ear
- mouth • tooth • arm • hand
- finger • thumb • leg • knee
- foot • toe • neck • shoulder
- back • stomach

b) Match.

1 head

Note

Irregular plurals

| one tooth | two teeth |
| one foot | two feet |

2 Listen and read

Toby: Goal! Yes!

Tim: Toby! Don't stand up! I can't see.

Dad: Please sit down, Toby!

Tim: Dad! My hands and feet are cold!

Dad: Well, put your hands in your pockets.

Toby: And jump up and down!

Amy: Hey, Toby. Look who's over there!

Dad: Don't point, Amy. It's rude.

Amy: But it's my teacher, Miss Kent. She's with her boyfriend!

Dad: Come on, you two. Don't be silly. Watch the match!

Now listen and repeat.

Everyday phrases
- Goal!   • Hey, Toby!
- Yes!   • Look who's over there!
- Well, ...   • It's rude.

3 Check

Right (✓) or wrong (✗)?

1 The children are at the cinema. ☒
2 Tim is cold. ☐
3 Amy's teacher is also there. ☐
4 Amy's teacher is with her sister. ☐

4  New words: Verbs

a) Listen and repeat.
- open • close • put • sit down
- stand up • point • touch • jump
- hold up • draw

b) Match.

1 *stand up*

Look and learn

Please **sit down**.
Please **don't stand up**.

5 Speak

a) Give an instruction to a friend.

Daniela, touch your head.

b) Now give two instructions.

Hannah, hold up your hand and point to the desk.

6  Rap

The Body Rap

Go to page 93 and listen and complete the rap.

Molly

Will

Mum

Rocco

Mr Giotto

1

Hurry up, Molly.

See you later, Mum!

OK! But don't go far. It's half past three.

Will and Molly Evans are on holiday with their parents in Italy.

Hello. Can you speak English?

Yes, I can, but I can't speak very well.

2

Are you Italian?

Yes, I am.

Look at the water!

Don't swim here. It's boring.

3

Can you dive?

Yes, we can.

And open your eyes under water?

Yes.

Good. Come on.

5

4

New words
- holiday   - far   - speak
- boring   - dive   - cave
- Wait.   - statue   - find
- queen   - surprise
- weekend

1 Listen and read

2 Check

Correct the sentences.

1 The children are in England.
   The children aren't in England. They're in Italy.
2 They're with their aunt and uncle.
3 Rocco is Spanish.
4 He can't speak English.
5 The statue is new.

3 Act

Learn the story and act it out.

51

25 Revision

1 Write what the people can and can't do.

1 Simon can play the guitar but he can't play the piano.
2 Kate can use a computer but she can't read a map very well.

	can	can't	not very well
1 Simon	(guitar)	(piano)	
2 Kate	(computer)		(map)
3 Jack	(chess)	(skateboard)	
4 Cara	(sailing boat)		(swimming)
5 Karen	(singing)	(horse riding)	

2 Do the food and drink crossword. Find the secret word.

Clues

orange ...   hot ...

mineral ...

banana ...

1	j	u	i	c	e
2					
3					
4					
5					
6					
7					
8					

3 Complete the conversation.

A: Can I ¹help you?
B: Yes, please. How ² ... are the ice creams?
A: ³ ... 85 pence.
B: What flavours ⁴ ... you got?
A: We've ⁵ ... vanilla, strawberry and chocolate.
B: ⁶ ... I have three strawberry ice creams, please?
A: Sure. ⁷ ... £2.55 pence, please.
B: Oh no! I've ⁸ ... got £2!

4 Label the picture.

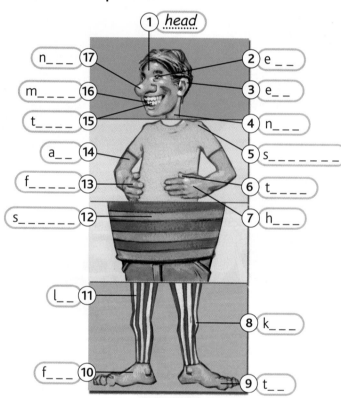

1 head
n___ 17
m____ 16
t____ 15
a__ 14
f_____ 13
s_____ 12
l__ 11
f___ 10

2 e _ _
3 e _ _
4 n___
5 s_____
6 t____
7 h___
8 k___
9 t_ _

5 🎧 Sounds fun / æ / and / ɑː /

a) Listen and repeat.
Look, there's Dan, in a van.
Can he drive it? Yes, he can.
Look, there's Mark, in a car.
He can't drive – he can't go far.

b) Listen again and underline the / æ / sounds in red and the / ɑː / sounds in green.

6 Chatterbox

Complete the conversation. Listen and practise with Toby. Then practise with a friend.

Hello! Can you swim?

Yes, I can.

I can't swim under water. Can you?

....

What sports can you play?

....

Can you jump up and down on one leg and sing a song in Russian?

....

Never mind! Bye! See you soon!

....

Toby

You

7 Game: Can you do it?

Play the game in pairs. You need a dice and two counters.

Rules

- Play in pairs.
- Throw a 1 or a 6 to start.
- If you land on a yellow or green square, follow the instructions.
- If you land on a picture square, say if you can or can't do what's in the picture. (3 = I can/can't sing.)
- The first person to reach FINISH is the winner.

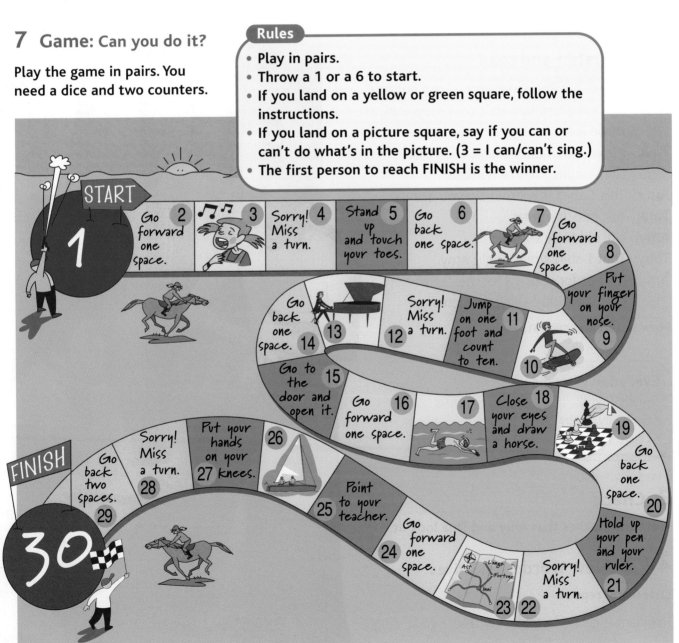

I don't like them.

1 🔊 New words:

Clothes

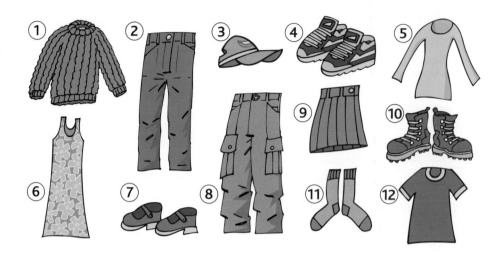

a) Listen and repeat.
- T-shirt • top • jumper
- jeans • trousers • skirt
- dress • socks • shoes
- boots • trainers
- baseball cap

b) Match.

1 jumper

2 🔊 Listen and read

Tina: Listen. It's Robbie Williams. He's brilliant.

Amy: Yes, I like him too. He's cool. Hey, look at those jeans.

Tina: Mmm. I don't like them. I don't like the sequins. They're horrible.

Amy: This T-shirt is wicked! Do you like it?

Tina: Yes, I do. It's great.

Amy: Uh, uh! Here's Toby.

Toby: That T-shirt's really ugly, Amy.

Amy: It's not for you, it's for me. Go away, Toby. Leave us alone.

Now listen and repeat.

> **Everyday phrases**
> - really [ugly]
> - Go away, [Toby].
> - Leave us alone.

3 Check

Note the clothes that Amy and Tina look at.

4 🔊 New words: Adjectives

Listen and repeat.

- brilliant • cool • horrible • wicked • great • ugly

Look and learn

I **like** the T-shirt. **I don't like** the jeans.

Do you like the T-shirt?   Yes, **I do.**
Do you like the jeans?   No, **I don't.**

I don't like = I do not like

Look and learn

I	→	me	You like **me**.
you	→	you	I like **you**.
he	→	him	I like **him**. (Robbie Williams)
she	→	her	I like **her**. (Britney Spears)
it	→	it	I like **it**. (the top)
we	→	us	They like **us**. (me and my sister)
you	→	you	I like **you**. (you and your friend)
they	→	them	I like **them**. (the jeans)

5 Speak

a) Talk about the clothes in Exercise 1.

I like the trainers. They're brilliant/wicked.
I don't like the shoes. They're horrible/ugly.

b) Ask your friend.

A: *Do you like the top?*
B: *Yes, I do. It's brilliant./No, I don't. It's horrible.*

6 Write

Complete the conversation with *me*, *you*, *him*, *her*, *it*, *us* or *them*.

A: Look at ¹*me*. Do you like my new baseball cap?
B: Yes, I like ² ...   a lot. I like orange and pink.
A: I've got a cap for ³ ... too. Here you are.
B: Oh thanks. Listen, this is Avril Lavigne.
A: I don't like ⁴ ... very much.
B: Oh, she's good. This is her new single.
A: Oh no! There's Eddie. Do you like ⁵ ... ?
B: He's OK.
C: Hello, you two. Yuk! Orange and pink baseball caps!
A: Huh! We like ⁶ ... . Go away, Eddie, and leave ⁷ ...
   alone.

7 Read and write

a) Read and note the clothes that Clara likes.

My favourite clothes ...

Clara from Cornwall.
My favourite clothes are jeans
and T-shirts or jumpers. I don't
like dresses or skirts. I've got
a new pair of jeans. I love
them. They're purple and
they've got silver and gold
sequins on them. I like trainers
and boots but I don't like shoes
very much. What about you?

b) Now write about your favourite clothes.

Portfolio

8 Song

The Clothes Song

Go to page 93 and listen and complete the song.

1 Read

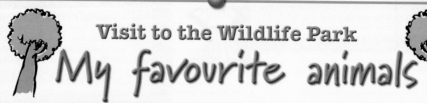

Visit to the Wildlife Park
My favourite animals

My favourite animals are chimpanzees. Chimpanzees are brown. They've got long arms and short legs. They live in rain forests in Africa. They eat plants, fruit and meat. At night they sleep in trees. They don't run fast. They walk, or climb trees and swing from tree to tree. Chimpanzees live for about 35 years. I like chimpanzees because they're clever.

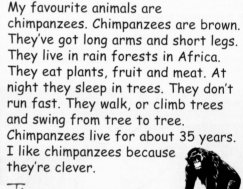

Tina

My favourite animals are tigers. Tigers are yellow and black. They've got big teeth. They live in the jungle in South Asia. They eat meat. They don't eat plants or fruit. They sleep in the day and hunt at night. They run very fast. Tigers live for about 20 years. I like tigers because they're beautiful.

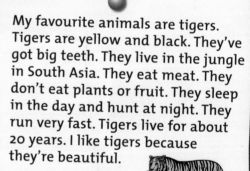

Mark

Now listen and repeat.

2 Check

Complete the details.

	Chimpanzees	Tigers
Colour:	...	yellow and black
Have got:	long arms and ...	big ...
Home:	...	the jungle
Food:	plants, ... and ...	...
Live for:	...	... years

3 🔊 New words: Verbs

Listen and repeat.

① live

② eat

③ sleep

④ hunt

⑤ run

⑥ walk

⑦ climb

⑧ swing

4 Write

Complete the sentences about tigers.

1 Tigers _are_ yellow and black.
2 They_'ve got_ big teeth.
3 They _live_ in the jungle.
4 They ... meat.
5 They ... plants or fruit.
6 They ... in the day.
7 They ... sleep at night.
8 At night they ... .
9 They ... fast.
10 They ... for about 20 years.

5 Speak

Ask questions about tigers and chimpanzees.

1 eat fruit and plants
2 sleep at night
3 run fast
4 live in rain forests
5 swing from tree to tree

A: *Do tigers eat plants and fruit?*
B: *No, they don't.*
A: *Do chimpanzees eat plants and fruit?*
B: *Yes, they do.*

6 🔊 Quiz

Listen to a radio quiz about giraffes.

a) Stop the recording after each question. Can you answer before Luke?

b) Listen again and note the information.

Colour:	_brown and yellow_
Have got:	...
Live:	...
Eat:	...
Sleep:	...

7 Write

a) Use your answers from Exercise 6 to write about giraffes.

Giraffes are brown and ... . They've got ... .

b) Write about your favourite animal for a school project.

My favourite animals are elephants. Elephants are grey. They ... .

8 🔊 Rap

The Animal Rap

Listen and complete. Then join in.

They ¹_hunt_ at night   They ⁴ ... from branches
And ² ... all day.   ⁵ ... up trees.
They ³ ... very fast   Their arms are ⁶ ...
To catch their prey.   They've got hairy knees.
They're tigers!   They're chimps!

57

28 He doesn't go to Hogwarts!

1  Read

Meet
Dan Radcliffe

Dan Radcliffe is an actor. He plays Harry Potter in the *Harry Potter* films. He lives with his parents in London. Here are the answers to the top five questions about Dan.

Where does Dan go to school?
He goes to a boys' school in London. He doesn't go to Hogwarts.

What time does he start and finish school?
He starts at twenty to nine and finishes at four o'clock. Then he does his homework.

What does he do in the holidays?
Dan loves the school holidays. He gets up late and has breakfast and lunch together! What does he do all day? He plays sport, does card tricks, plays computer games and watches television. One of his favourite programmes is *The Simpsons*. He goes to bed at ten o'clock.

Does he like chips?
No, he doesn't. He likes fish but he doesn't like chips. For breakfast he has fruit juice, cereal and a cup of hot chocolate. His favourite snack is diet cola and a chocolate bar!

What music does he like?
He likes punk and rock. His favourite bands are the Sex Pistols, ERM and U2. He plays the bass guitar but he isn't very good!

Now listen and repeat.

2 Check

Right (✓) or wrong (✗)?

1 Dan is Harry Potter in the films. ✓
2 His school is Hogwarts. ☐
3 He has got a computer. ☐
4 His bedtime is nine o'clock. ☐
5 His favourite snack is diet cola and a chocolate bar. ☐
6 He has got a guitar. ☐

3  New words: ①

Daily routine

a) Listen and repeat.
- get up
- have breakfast
- go to school
- start school ②
- have lunch
- have dinner
- finish school ③
- do homework
- go to bed
- watch TV
- play computer games ④
- play sport

b) Match.
1 have breakfast

58

Look and learn

Dan go**es** to school in London.
He **doesn't go** to Hogwarts!

Dan get**s** up late.
He **doesn't get** up early.

Dan ha**s** fruit juice for breakfast.
He **doesn't have** coffee.

4 Write

Complete the sentences about Dan with the correct form of these verbs.

| • have • go • not go • start • watch |
| • do • get up • finish • live • play |

1 Dan *lives* with his parents.
2 He ... to a boys' school in London.
3 He ... to Hogwarts.
4 He ... school at twenty to nine and ... at four o'clock.
5 After school he ... his homework.
6 In the holidays he ... late.
7 He ... television and ... computer games.
8 He ... a cup of hot chocolate for breakfast.

⑤

⑨

⑥

⑩

⑦

⑪

⑧

⑫

Look and learn

Does Dan **like** fish?   Yes, he **does**.
Does he **like** chips?   No, he **doesn't**.

5 Speak

Ask and answer about Dan.

A: *Does Dan go to school in London?*
B: *Yes, he does.*

• go to school in London • go to Hogwarts
• get up early in the holidays • play sport
• like chips • have fruit juice for breakfast
• like *The Simpsons* • play the piano

Look and learn

Where **does** he **go** to school?
What time **does** he **get** up?
What **does** he **do** all day?

6 Speak

a) Ask and answer about Rupert Grint, the actor who plays Ron Weasley in the *Harry Potter* films.

A: *Where does Rupert go to school?*
B: *He goes to a school near London.*

1 Where/go to school? (near London)
2 What time/get up? (7.30)
3 What/have for breakfast? (eggs on toast)
4 What time/start school? (8.45)
5 What/do after school? (homework/play rap music)
6 What time/go to bed? (9.00)

b) Use the questions to ask your friend.

A: *Where do you go to school, Matteus?*
B: *I go to ...*

7 Write

Write about your friend's school day for a school website. Look at Exercise 1.

Matteus goes to ... school in ... .

8  Song

Vicky the Vampire

Go to page 94 and listen and complete the song.

29

My school day

1 Read

Listen and read the articles about Rob and Melanie.

Rob

I'm Rob. I'm eleven years old and I go to Aston Secondary School in Oxford. I'm in Year 7. My favourite subjects are Maths and Science.

I start school at 8.50 in the morning. There are four lessons before lunch and two after lunch. Lunch is at 12.30. I have lunch in the school cafeteria.

I start lessons again in the afternoon at 1.30 and finish school at 3.30. From 3.30 to 4.30 I go to Homework Club and do my homework. On Tuesday and Thursday I play football after school.

Melanie

Melanie is eleven years old. She goes to Columbus Elementary School in Forest Lake, Minnesota. She's in the sixth grade. Her favourite subjects are Spanish and History.

She starts school at 8 and she has six lessons a day. She has lunch at 12 in the school cafeteria. After lunch there is a study period from 12.30 to 1.30 and Melanie does her homework then. Lessons start again at 1.45. She finishes at three. On Wednesday after school she plays in the school band and on Thursday she does basketball.

New words
- secondary school
- in the morning · before
- cafeteria · again
- in the afternoon
- elementary school · grade
- study period · basketball

2 New words: School subjects

a) Listen and repeat.
- English · Maths (Mathematics) · History · Geography · Science
- French · Spanish · I.C.T. (Information and Communication Technology)
- Drama · Art · Domestic Science · R.E. (Religious Education)
- P.E. (Physical Education) · Games

b) **What are your favourite subjects?**

3 Check

a) Read about Rob and Melanie again and complete the chart.

	Rob	Melanie	Harry
Starts school	8.50	...	...
Number of lessons	...	6	...
Favourite subjects	Maths, Science	...	...
Has lunch	...	12.00	...
Starts afternoon lessons	1.30	...	...
Finishes school	...	3.00	...
Does homework	...	12.30 – 1.30	...
After school activities (e.g. sport, music)	plays football on Tuesday and Thursday	...	...

b) Compare Rob's and Melanie's school day.

Rob starts school at 8.50 but Melanie starts school at 8.

4 🔲 Listen

Listen to Harry and complete the details of his school day in the chart in Exercise 3.

5 Speak

Your partner is from the UK or the USA. He/She asks about your school.

1 **A:** *What time do you start school?*
  B: *I start at ... .*

1 What time do you start school?
2 What time is lunch?
3 Are there lessons in the afternoon?
4 Is there a Homework Club?
5 What do you do after school?

Project

My school day

Writing tip

Capital letters (2)

We use capital letters for:
- Days of the week *Tuesday*
- Languages and nationalities *French, Italian*
- School subjects on a timetable *Maths, Geography*

Read about the people in Exercise 1 again and find examples of capital letters.

Portfolio Write

Write an article about your school day. Use Rob's article to help you.

Paragraph 1
- How old are you?
- What school do you go to?
- What year are you in?
- What are your favourite subjects?

Paragraph 2
- What time do you start school in the morning?
- How many lessons are there every day?
- What time do you have lunch and where do you have it?

Paragraph 3
- Are there lessons in the afternoon?
- What time do you finish school?
- What do you do after school?
- When and where do you do your homework?

I'm ... . I'm ... years old. I go to ... Elementary School in Argentina. I'm in the 6th grade. My favourite subjects at school are ...

1 Do the adjective crossword. Find the secret word.

What's the secret word?

h
o
r
r
i
b
l
e

Clues

1 I hate it. It's h... .
2 I like s... hair.
3 London is a b... city.
4 It isn't pretty. It's u... .
5 The opposite of 3 is s... .
6 That T-shirt is w... . It's really cool!
7 I like Robbie Williams. He's g... !
8 A chimpanzee has got l... arms.
9 The opposite of 4 is b... .

The secret word is ... .

2 Replace the underlined words with the words in the box.

• us • you • it • her • them • him

1 I like those trousers.   I like *them*.
2 She likes you and your brother.   She likes ... .
3 I like Mr Vialli.   I like ... .
4 He likes Tina.   He likes ... .
5 I like your skateboard.   I like ... .
6 They like my brother and me.   They like ... .

3 Complete with do or don't.

A: ¹*Do* you like those boots?
B: Yes, I ²... . They're wicked! But I ³... like that T-shirt. ⁴... you like it?
A: No, I ⁵... . It's horrible.
B: Look! There's Miss Todd and her daughter. ⁶... they live here?
A: Yes, they ⁷... . They live in Elm Road.

4 Look at the chart. Write sentences about the animals.

Tigers live in India. They eat meat. They hunt at night. Giraffes live in Africa. They eat leaves. They don't hunt at night.

Animal		Habitat	Food	Hunt at night?
	Tigers	India	meat	✓
	Giraffes	Africa	leaves	✗
	Chimpanzees	rain forests	fruit	✗
	Ostriches	Australia	meat and leaves	✓

30

5 Choose the right words.

- gets up   • doesn't   • read   • plays   • loves
- doesn't like   • does   • goes   • has   • watches
- watch   • does   • don't   • go

Carl is mad about basketball. He ¹*doesn't like* football but he ²... basketball. He ³... at seven o'clock, he ⁴... a big breakfast and then he ⁵... to school. He ⁶... go home after school. He ⁷... basketball with his school friends. Then they ⁸... home together. What ⁹... he do at home in the evening? He ¹⁰... his homework and then he ¹¹... basketball on the television. Do his parents ¹²... sports? No, they ¹³... . They ¹⁴... books.

6 Sounds fun / g / and / dʒ /

a) Listen and repeat.

Gary's orange jumper
Looks great with his jeans.
And Joe's green T-shirt
Looks good when it's clean!

b) Listen again and underline the / g / sounds in red and the / dʒ / sounds in green.

7 Chatterbox

Complete the conversation. Listen and practise with Tina. Then practise with a friend.

Hi! I like your clothes today.

Thanks.

Do you like this song?

....

Her name's Leah Lovett. She's new. I like her. Do you like Robbie Williams?

....

I think he's wicked. What about bands? Who do you like?

....

Are they new? I don't know them.

....

It's late. Bye now!

....

Tina

You

8 Game: Clothes Puzzle

What's the secret code?

a) Write the names of the clothes in the boxes. Then look at the numbers above the letters and find out which letter each number stands for.

b) What are these clothes?

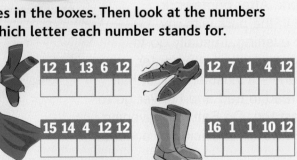

5	8	2	18	4	14

12	1	13	6	12

12	7	1	4	12

10	1	18

12	6	3	14	10

15	14	4	12	12

16	1	1	10	12

5	4	9	11	12

10	14	9	3	11	4	14	12

10	-	12	7	3	14	10

10	14	1	8	12	4	14	12

We always walk home together.

1 🔲 **Read**

Read Mark's page on his school website.

Everyday phrases
I'm good at [sports].
[I'm] late for [school].
[He lives] next door.
[I read] in bed.

Welcome to Mark's Page

Back Forward Stop Refresh Home AutoFill Print Mail

Address: @ http://www.myhomepage.co.uk/markspage.htm   › go

Favorites History Search Scrapbook Page Holder

Mark's Page

Hello!

Hi everybody. Welcome to my page!
My name is Mark Vialli and I'm in Year 9
at Clifton Park School!

Good things about me

I'm good at sports and I like football very
much. I'm always happy and I laugh a lot.

Bad things about me

I'm often late for school and I'm sometimes
bored in class!

My free time

I usually walk home from school with Toby.
He lives next door. I sometimes go to his
house and have a snack. Then I go home
and do my homework. After homework
I often play football in the park with my
friends. Later in the evening, I usually go to
my room and play games on my computer.
I never go to bed early – it's usually about half
past nine. I always read in bed and I never go to
sleep before half past ten. On Saturday evening,
my sister and I often watch television or a video.

Internet zone

Now listen and repeat.

31

2 🔊 New words:

Everyday activities

a) Listen and repeat.

• walk home • have a snack
• read in bed • go to sleep
• watch a video • play football
• play cards • listen to music
• meet friends • go to bed

b) Match.

1 watch a video

3 Check

Write the activities in order.

1 b) Mark walks home from school.

a) plays football
b) walks home from school
c) does homework
d) reads in bed
e) has a snack
f) plays computer games
g) goes to bed

Look and learn

always	usually	often	sometimes	never

I **usually read** in bed. He **always reads** in bed.

I**'m usually** happy. She**'s never** happy.

4 Write

Put the word in brackets in the right place.

1 Amy is never late for school.

1 Amy is late for school. (never)
2 Banjo goes to bed late. (often)
3 Tim is hungry. (always)
4 Toby goes to Mark's house after school. (sometimes)
5 Amy and Tina do their homework together. (usually)

5 Speak and write

a) Tick the right box and talk about you.

I'm sometimes late for school.

School Quiz!

How often are you:
1 late for school?
2 hungry at school?
3 bored in class?

How often do you:
4 walk home from school?
5 watch a video after school?
6 read a school book in bed?

	always	usually	often	sometimes	never

b) Now ask a friend and tick the right box. Use a different colour.

A: *How often are you late for school?*
B: *I'm sometimes late for school.*

c) Write about your friend.

Rita is sometimes late for school.
She never walks home from school.

6 Write

Write your own page for a school website.
Write about some good and bad things
about you, and what you do in your free time.

32 What are you doing?

1 🎧 Listen and read

Amy: Hello. 07790 62371.

Tina: Hi, Amy. It's Tina. What are you doing?

Amy: I'm doing my English homework. I'm writing a story. Where are you?

Tina: I'm in the park with Mark and Dad.

Amy: What's Mark doing?

Tina: He's playing football with his friends.

Amy: Are you playing, too?

Tina: Don't be daft. I'm taking a photo for our school project.

Amy: Don't drop the camera!

Now listen and repeat.

Everyday phrases
Hello. (07790 62371).
It's [Tina].
Don't be daft.

Note!
07790 = Oh-double seven-
          nine-oh

2 Check

Right (✓) or wrong (✗)?

1 Amy has got some
   English homework.   ✓
2 Tina is at home.   ☐
3 Mark is in the park.   ☐
4 Tina hasn't got a camera.   ☐

3 New words: Everyday activities 2

a) Listen and repeat.

- write an email • talk to a friend • have a shower
- make a sandwich • listen to the radio
- do my homework • write a story • take a photo
- wash the car

b) Match.

1 do my homework

Look and learn

What **are you doing**?
I'm writing a story.
What **is he/she doing**?
He's/She's playing football.

Note
do/do**ing** play/play**ing**
write/writ**ing** sit/si**tt**ing

4 Speak

Talk about the people in the pictures in Exercise 3.

1 A: *What's he doing?*
  B: *He's doing his homework.*
2 A: *What's she doing?*
  B: *She's ... .*

Look and learn

Are you doing your homework?
Yes, I am./No, I'm not.

Is he/she playing football?
Yes, **he/she is**. No, **he/she isn't**.

5 Game

Choose one of the activities in Exercise 3. Act it. Don't speak. Your partner must guess what you are doing.

A: *Are you making a sandwich?*
B: *No, I'm not./Yes, I am.*

6 Read and write

a) Complete Tina's email to a friend.

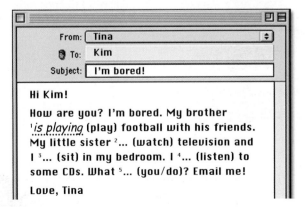

From: Tina
To: Kim
Subject: I'm bored!

Hi Kim!

How are you? I'm bored. My brother ¹ *is playing* (play) football with his friends. My little sister ²... (watch) television and I ³... (sit) in my bedroom. I ⁴... (listen) to some CDs. What ⁵... (you/do)? Email me!

Love, Tina

b) Write to Tina and tell her what you are doing.

67

33 The sun is shining.

1 🔘 New words:

The weather

Listen and repeat.

① It's hot. ② It's cold. ③ It's warm. ④ It's raining. ⑤ It's foggy.

⑥ It's sunny./ The sun is shining. ⑦ It's cloudy. ⑧ It's windy. ⑨ It's snowing.

Look and learn

What's the weather like?
It's warm and sunny.
The sun's shining.

2 Speak

a) Say what the weather is like in the different cities.

1 A: *What's the weather like in London?*
   B: *It's cloudy.*

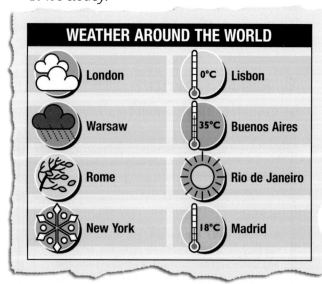

WEATHER AROUND THE WORLD

	London		0°C	Lisbon
	Warsaw		35°C	Buenos Aires
	Rome			Rio de Janeiro
	New York		18°C	Madrid

b) Ask and say what the weather is like today.

A: *What's the weather like today?*
B: *It's ... .*

3 🔘 Read

Amy and Toby get a postcard from their American friends, Matt and Lisa.

Dear Amy and Toby,
   We're on holiday in Florida for a week. We're staying with our aunt and uncle. The weather is very hot and I'm sitting next to the swimming pool. I'm wearing my new sunglasses. They're really cool! Mom and Dad are shopping in town and Matt is swimming in the pool. What's the weather like in Bristol? Is it raining?
   Love,
   Lisa (and Matt)

Amy a
97 Sou
Bristo
BR28
U.K.

Now listen and repeat.

4 Check

Answer the questions.

1 Where are Lisa and Matt?
2 What's the weather like there?
3 What is Lisa wearing?
4 Where are Matt's parents?
5 What is Matt doing?

Look and learn

What are you and Matt doing?
We're swimming in the pool.

What are your parents doing?
They're shopping in town.

5 Act

Telephone one of the people in the pictures below.

A: *Hello.*
B: *Hi, Emma. It's Sofia. Where are you?*
A: *We're on holiday in Italy.*
B: *What's the weather like?*
A: *It's sunny.*
B: *What are you doing at the moment?*
A: *We're having lunch.*

① Emma and Robin / Italy / have lunch

② Sue and David / London / sit in a café

③ Ron and his brother / Scotland / play computer games

6 Write

Write what the people in Exercise 5 are doing.

1 Emma and Robin are on holiday in Italy. It's sunny and they're having lunch.

7 🔊 Listen

Listen to three conversations and choose the correct postcard.

A

B

C

8 Write

You are on holiday in your country. Write a postcard to Toby or Amy.

- Where are you?
- Who are you staying with?
- What's the weather like?
- What are you doing?

9 🔊 Rap

The Weather Rap

Go to page 94 and listen and complete the rap.

Shop detectives

 Cathy

 Dylan

 Aunt Helen

 Uncle Jack

 Laura

 Man

A day in high summer.

1

2 Hi, Aunt Helen! It's Cathy. We're sitting on the train.

Where are you?

We're very near London.

3 Great! I'm standing in the station outside the café.

4 Hi, Aunt Helen!

Hello, you two! Lovely to see you.

Where's Uncle Jack?

He's at work. Come on. He's waiting to see you.

5

Uncle Jack is a store detective in a big London store.

Hello! Come in.

Hello, Uncle Jack. What are you doing?

6 I'm watching people in the store.

Cool!

70

New words
- high summer • train • outside
- café • lovely • at work • store
- people • detective • department
- coat • lift • Well done! • job

1 🔊 **Listen and read**

2 Check

Answer the questions.

1 Where are Cathy and Dylan in Picture 2?
2 Where is Aunt Helen standing?
3 What is Uncle Jack's job?
4 What is the man wearing?
5 What is he doing?

3 Act

Learn the story and act it out.

35 Revision

1 Complete each phrase with *a*, *an*, *the*, *to* or nothing, if no word is needed.

1 play / football   *play football*
2 have / shower   *have a shower*
3 go / bed
4 listen / music
5 wash / car
6 have / snack
7 take / photo
8 talk / Toby
9 go / home
10 write / email

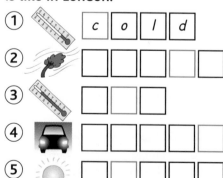

2 Tick the correct places for the adverbs.

1 He ᵃ☑ reads ᵇ☐ in bed. (always)
2 She ᵃ☐ does ᵇ☐ her homework at school. (usually)
3 They ᵃ☐ are ᵇ☐ late for school. (never)
4 John ᵃ☐ plays ᵇ☐ football after school. (sometimes)
5 I ᵃ☐ am ᵇ☐ bored at home. (often)
6 We ᵃ☐ watch ᵇ☐ television before breakfast. (never)

3 What's the weather like?

Write the words in the spaces. Then unscramble all the red letters to find out what the weather is like in London.

① | c | o | l | d |
②
③
④
⑤
⑥

The weather in London is ☐☐☐☐☐☐.

4 Complete the gaps with the present continuous form of the verbs in brackets.

Dave: Hi, Sue. It's Dave here. ¹*Are you having* .... (have) lunch?
Sue: No, we aren't. It's only twelve o'clock.
Dave: What ²... you all ... ? (do)
Sue: Mum ³... (have) a shower, Dad ⁴... (sit) in the garden and I ⁵... (play) games on my computer.
Dave: Where are Lucy and Holly?
Sue: They ⁶... (wash) Dad's car. It's hot here. ⁷... the sun ... (shine) in Scotland?
Dave: No, it isn't. It ⁸... (rain) here.
Sue: What ⁹... you ... (do)?
Dave: I ¹⁰... (make) some sandwiches.

5 🔊 Sounds fun / tʃ / and / ʃ /

a) Listen and repeat.
Charlie is washing his hair in the shower,
Shirley is playing chess with Archie
And Sharon is learning Chinese.

b) Listen again and underline the / tʃ / sounds in red and the / ʃ / sounds in green.

6 🎧 Chatterbox

Complete the conversation. Listen and practise with Toby. Then practise with a friend.

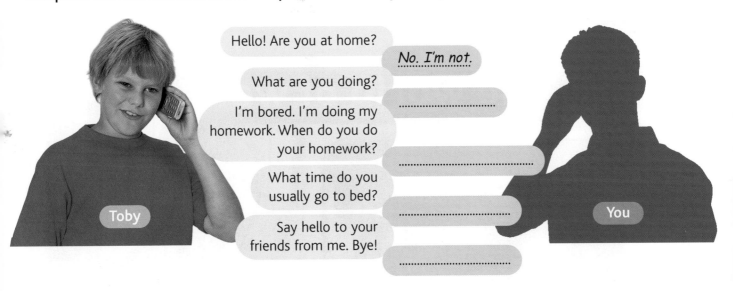

Toby: Hello! Are you at home?
You: No. I'm not.
Toby: What are you doing?
You: ....
Toby: I'm bored. I'm doing my homework. When do you do your homework?
You: ....
Toby: What time do you usually go to bed?
You: ....
Toby: Say hello to your friends from me. Bye!
You: ....

7 Game: Spot the difference

Play the game in pairs. Look at the pictures. Find seven differences.

1 *In picture A the girl is wearing a red top, but in picture B she's wearing a green top.*

Spot the difference

73

He's a mechanic.

1  **Read**

The world of work

① Celia teaches in a school in Scotland. In this photo she's teaching Maths.

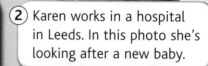

② Karen works in a hospital in Leeds. In this photo she's looking after a new baby.

③ John works in a garage in York. In this photo he's repairing a sports car.

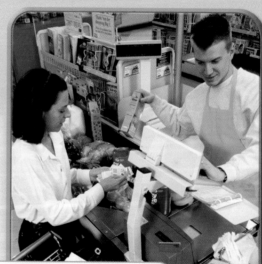

④ Tony works in a supermarket in Bristol. In this photo he's serving a customer.

2 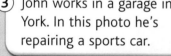 **New words: Work**

a) Listen and repeat.

- waiter · teacher · doctor · mechanic · nurse
- shop assistant · secretary · dentist
- bus driver · chef

- office · hospital · supermarket
- restaurant · school · garage

- repair · look after · cook · teach · serve
- type · work

b) Match the people in Exercise 1 with their jobs.

1 Celia's a teacher.

Look and learn

I work in a garage. In this photo I'm repairing a car.

He works in a garage.
In this photo he's repairing a car.

3 Speak

a) Talk about the people's jobs.

1 A: *What's Celia's job?*
 B: *She's a teacher.*
 A: *Where does she work?*
 B: *She works in a school.*

b) Say what the people are doing in the photos.

1 A: *What's Celia doing in the photo?*
 B: *She's teaching Maths.*

4 Game

What's my job?

Choose one of the jobs in Exercise 2 and mime it. The others must guess what your job is. They can only ask four questions.

A: *Watch!*
B: *Are you holding a book?*
A: *No, I'm not.*
C: *Are you serving food?*
A: *Yes, I am.*
D: *Do you work in a restaurant?*
A: *Yes, I do.*
B: *You're a waiter.*

5 Listen

Listen and write where the people work.

1 John works in a ... . He's a ... .
2 Anna ... .
3 Sophie ... .

6 Song

The Job Song

Go to page 94 and listen and complete the song.

7 Write

Complete the conversation with the correct form of the verb.

Amy: Hello, Mrs Vialli. Is Tina in?
Mrs V: Yes, she's in the shower. She [1] *'s washing* her hair. (wash)
Amy: What? Again?
Mrs V: Yes, she [2] ... her hair every day. (wash)
Amy: OK. What [3] ... ? (Mark/do) [4] ... football? (he/play)
Mrs V: Yes, he is. He always [5] ... football after school on Friday. (play)
Amy: What time [6] ... finish? (he/finish)
Mrs V: At 5.30. He usually [7] ... home at six. (come)

8 Write

Write about the person in the picture. Use these words.

Dino is a chef. He ... . In this ...

• chef
• restaurant
• New York
• make
• pizza

37 My birthday's on August 1st.

1 🔊 New words: Months of the year

Listen and repeat the months of the year.

January	February
March	April
May	June
July	August
September	October
November	December

2 Speak

Tell the class.

My favourite months are ... and ... . I don't like ... or ... .

3 🔊 Ordinal numbers

a) Go to page 95 and listen and repeat the ordinal numbers.

b) Say these ordinal numbers.

3rd	14th	1st	23rd
2nd	28th	31st	6th

4 🔊 Listen

Listen and write the dates.

1 April 5th

5 Speak

Ask about the months of the year.

A: *What's the sixth month of the year?*
B: *It's June.*

6 🔊 Listen and read

Amy: What day is it today?
Tina: It's Monday.
Amy: What's the date?
Tina: It's May 14th. It's my dad's birthday on Thursday.
Amy: My birthday is in August.
Tina: When?
Amy: On August 1st. When's your birthday?
Tina: Guess.
Amy: Don't be silly! I don't know.
Tina: It's on December 23rd!
Amy: It's two days before Christmas. Bad luck!
Tina: It's OK. I get birthday presents on December 23rd and Christmas presents on December 25th!

Now listen and repeat.

Everyday phrases
• Guess.
• I don't know.
• Bad luck!

76

Look and learn

When's your birthday?
It's **on** December 23rd.

7 Check

Answer the questions with a date.

1 What's the date today?
2 When's Mr Vialli's birthday?
3 When's Amy's birthday?
4 When's Tina's birthday?
5 When is Christmas?

8 Speak

a) Look at Amy's birthday calendar. Ask and say when the birthdays are.

A: *When is her dad's birthday?*
B: *It's on ... .*

JANUARY	FEBRUARY	MARCH
January 8th: Dad		March 2nd: Toby

APRIL	MAY	JUNE
		June 17th: Tim

JULY	AUGUST	SEPTEMBER
	August 1st: Me	

OCTOBER	NOVEMBER	DECEMBER
October 1st: Mum		December 23rd Tina

b) Talk about you and your family's birthdays.

A: *When's your birthday?*
B: *It's on ... . What about you?*
A: *My birthday is on ... . When's your mum's birthday?*
B: *It's on ... . When's your ... ?*

9 Write

Write about your favourite day of the year.

My favourite day is ... because it's ... .

38 It's next to the café.

1 🔘 New words:

Places in town

a) Listen and repeat.

- station • computer shop
- book shop • cinema
- record shop • newsagent
- supermarket • car park
- bus stop • pet shop
- café • swimming pool

b) Match.

1 cinema

2 🔘 Listen and read

Mr Scott: Let's meet here in front of the Planetarium at three o'clock.

Toby: OK. See you later, Dad.

Tina: Where's the record shop? I want to buy a CD for Dad's birthday.

Amy: It's next to the café, over there.

Toby: Let's go to the computer shop, Mark.

Mark: OK. Good idea. Where is it?

Toby: Opposite the cinema.

Mark: Cool.

Now listen and repeat.

Everyday phrases
- [It's] over there.
- Good idea.

Look and learn

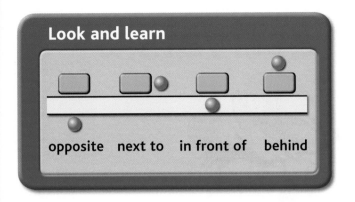

opposite   next to   in front of   behind

3 Act

a) You are in the town below. Ask and say where places are.

1 the computer shop   2 the bus stop
3 the cinema   4 the school

1 A: *Excuse me, where's the computer shop?*
   B: *It's in West Street, opposite the newsagent.*

b) Now ask about the other places on the map.

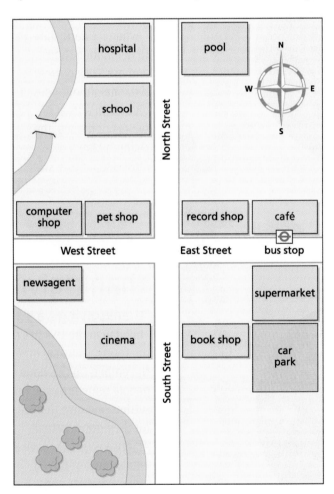

Look and learn

Let's go to the computer shop.
I **want to** play some computer games.

5 Speak

a) Match the places with the things you can do there.

1 d) cinema – see the new James Bond film

1	cinema	a)	buy some food
2	café	b)	buy a magazine
3	newsagent	c)	have a drink
4	supermarket	d)	see the new James Bond film
5	record shop	e)	play some computer games
6	computer shop	f)	buy a CD

b) Ask and say what you want to do.

A: *Let's go to a computer shop. I want to play some computer games.*
B: *OK. Good idea./Sorry, I can't, I'm busy.*

6 Read and write

a) Read Amy's message to a friend, Linda.

Hi Linda!
   Let's go shopping on Saturday morning. I want to buy Justin Timberlake's new CD. There's a really good record shop next to the café. Please come!
     Love from
        Amy

b) Now send a message to a friend. Say where you want to go, what you want to buy and where the shop is.

4  Rap

The Map Rap

Go to page 94 and listen and join in the rap.

79

39 Famous festivals

Happy Christmas!

1 🔈 Read

Listen and read about famous festivals.

Christmas Day

Christmas Day is on December 25th. British people usually have a Christmas tree in their house and put lights and decorations on it. On Christmas Eve, the day before Christmas Day, children put stockings by their beds for presents and open them on Christmas Day. The traditional Christmas dinner is turkey and Christmas pudding.

Halloween

Halloween is on October 31st. In the UK and the USA children wear fancy dress. When it's dark, they go to neighbours' houses and ask 'Trick or treat?'. If the neighbour doesn't give them a treat of sweets or money, the children play a trick. Most people give sweets.

Easter

Easter is in March or April. It starts on Good Friday. British people often eat hot cross buns on this day. Easter Sunday is a favourite day for children because they get chocolate Easter eggs. Parents sometimes hide Easter eggs in the garden and the children look for them. The traditional lunch on Easter Sunday is lamb.

Thanksgiving

Thanksgiving is a big holiday in the USA. It's on the fourth Thursday in November. On this day, people remember the first settlers and give thanks for their good fortune. Americans usually have a family meal of turkey, sweet potatoes and pumpkin pie.

New words

• festival • tree lights
• decorations • stockings
• traditional • turkey • pudding
• hot cross buns • hide
• look for • lamb • fancy dress
• dark • play a trick • treat
• most • remember
• settlers • fortune • meal
• sweet potatoes • pumpkin pie

2 Check

Answer the questions.

1 What is the name of the day before Christmas Day?
2 When do British children open their Christmas presents?
3 When do children get Easter eggs?
4 When do they eat hot cross buns?
5 What do children wear at Halloween?
6 Is a 'treat' good or bad?
7 Is Thanksgiving a British or an American festival?
8 What is the Thanksgiving meal?

3 Listen

Listen to three songs and rhymes. Match each song or rhyme with a festival.

1 *Easter*

4 Speak

**Bring to class a photo of a special day in your country.
Say who is in the photo and what is happening.**

Project Portfolio

Festivals in my country

Writing tip

Dates
We write:
October 31st or 31st October,

but we say:
*October the thirty-first or
the thirty-first of October.*

Say the dates in the texts in Exercise 1.

Write and say the date today.

Write

Design a poster giving information about a festival in your country.

• What's the name of the festival?
• What date is it?
• What do people do?
• What do they wear?
• What do they eat?
• Do they give presents?

Valentine's Day

Valentine's Day is on
14th February. People send
romantic or funny cards
to people that they like.
They don't usually sign their
names. They sometimes give...

81

Revision

1 **Write about the people and their jobs.**

1 She's a nurse. She works in a hospital.

① ② ③ ④ ⑤ ⑥

2 **Choose the correct verb phrases.**

1 My brother *works*/*is working* at home this morning.
2 A nurse *usually works*/*is usually working* in a hospital.
3 I *watch*/*'m watching* a good film on television at the moment.
4 He's a mechanic. He *repairs*/ *'s repairing* cars and motorbikes.
5 Sorry I can't come. I *cook*/*'m cooking* lunch.
6 My mother never *teaches*/*is teaching* on Saturday.

3 **Complete the table.**

We write	We say
January 9th	*January the ninth*
November 3rd	November the third
August 4th	...
...	July the first
April 2nd	...
May 31st	...
...	March the twenty-third

4 **Choose the correct words.**

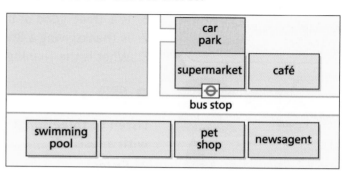

1 The supermarket is *next to*/*opposite* the café.
2 The bus stop is *behind*/*in front of* the supermarket.
3 The newsagent is *next to*/*opposite* the café.
4 The swimming pool is *next to*/*near* the pet shop.
5 The car park is *in front of*/*behind* the supermarket.

5 **Write the words in three groups.**

• computer shop • chef • June • station
• March • bus driver • restaurant • May
• dentist • garage • October • nurse

places	people	months
computer shop	*chef*	*June*

6 **Match the places with the activities. Then write sentences.**

1 Let's go to the computer shop. I want to play some computer games.

Ⓐ have a cola Ⓑ play some computer games Ⓒ watch television

Ⓓ buy some food Ⓔ look at the animals Ⓕ see Star Wars

7 Sounds fun

/ ɔː / and / ɜː /

a) Listen and repeat.
Paul's birthday is on
August the fourth.
He's fourteen on Thursday.
Happy birthday, Paul.

**b) Listen again and underline
the / ɔː / sounds in red and
the / ɜː / sounds in green.**

8 Chatterbox

**Complete the conversation. Listen and practise with Dan. Then
practise with a friend.**

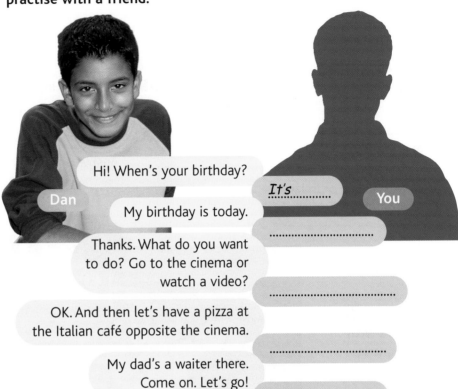

Dan: Hi! When's your birthday?

You: It's ....

Dan: My birthday is today.

You: ....

Dan: Thanks. What do you want
to do? Go to the cinema or
watch a video?

You: ....

Dan: OK. And then let's have a pizza at
the Italian café opposite the cinema.

You: ....

Dan: My dad's a waiter there.
Come on. Let's go!

You: ....

9 Game: Crossword

Complete the crossword.

CLUES ACROSS

2 3rd month of the year (5)
6 He or she works in a hospital. (6)
7 One man, two … (3)
9 I like Tina. She's n… . (4)
12 This person works in an office. (9)

CLUES DOWN

1 What time do you go to … at night? (3)
2 A … repairs cars. (8)
3 My favourite … in the house is the kitchen. (4)
4 Opposite of *she*. (2)
5 The first month of the year. (7)
7 What's your name? … name is Toby. (2)
8 He or she looks after people in a hospital. (5)
10 This person cooks food in a restaurant. (4)
11 Fifth month of the year. (3)

The English language

1 Read

Listen and read about the English language.

English is the first language of about 375 million people. The main English-speaking countries are the UK, the Republic of Ireland, the USA, Canada, South Africa, Australia and New Zealand.

New words
- New Zealand
- the Republic of Ireland
- South Africa

2 Speak

Look at the map and match the numbers with the countries.

Number one is Canada.

Australia
Canada
New Zealand
the Republic of Ireland
the UK
the USA
South Africa

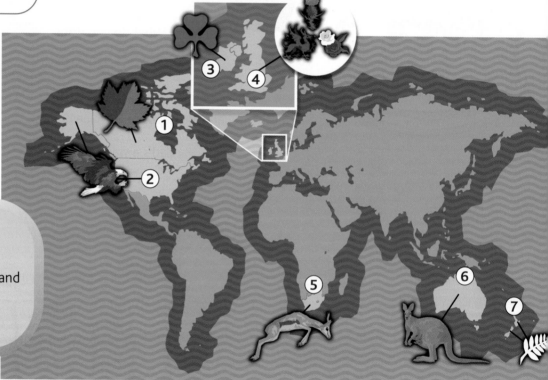

3 Listen

Listen and say where the children are from.

1 *Adam is from South Africa.*

(1) Adam

(2) Carrie

(3) Dean

(4) Vicki

84

4 Speak

Many words in English are similar in other languages. Which words do you know?

I know 'television', 'telephone' ... .

 ① television (TV) ② radio ③ music

 ④ telephone ⑤ video

⑥ film star

 ⑦ pop star ⑧ bus

 ⑨ cinema ⑩ sport ⑪ football

 ⑫ hamburger

⑭ taxi

⑬ jeans

 ⑮ tennis ⑯ hotel ⑰ walkman

Project

Portfolio

Find examples of English words in your language. Look at newspapers, magazines and signs. Make a poster.

ENGLISH IN MY COUNTRY

video   music
taxi   bus
POP STAR
jeans
CINEMA
film star   hotel
SPORT   hamburger

Castles

1 🎧 Read

Listen and read about Harlech Castle.

Harlech Castle WALES

Harlech Castle is a famous old castle in the North of Wales. It is on a rock. From the castle there is a beautiful view of the mountains and the sea. The castle is over seven hundred years old.

The castle is square. There are four main towers and a wall. In the castle there is a big hall called the Great Hall, a kitchen, store rooms and a chapel. Upstairs there are bedrooms and living rooms. In the four towers there are also bedrooms. There is a long staircase from the castle to the bottom of the rock. Today there isn't any sea at the bottom of the rock.

Harlech Castle is one of the three top castles for tourists to Wales.

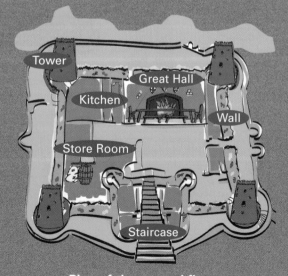

Plan of the ground floor.

New words

- castle - famous - Wales - rock - view
- mountains - sea - over - square - main
- tower - wall - hall - store room - chapel
- upstairs - staircase - bottom - top - tourist

2 Check

Right (✓) or wrong (✗)?

1 Harlech Castle is in Wales. ✓

2 It's five hundred years'old. ✗

3 There are two towers in Harlech Castle. ☐

4 There are bedrooms upstairs. ☐

5 There is a staircase to the bottom of the rock. ✓

6 Harlech Castle isn't interesting for tourists. ☐

3 Listen

Daisy and Sean are on a school visit to Harlech Castle. Listen and find out where they are.

Are they:

- in the Great Hall? - on a tower? - in the chapel?

4 Speak

Say where there are castles in your country.

There's an old castle in ... . It's called ... . It is ... years old.

Study tip

Learning new words (2)

Sometimes you can remember new words if you draw pictures.

Find three words in the text and draw a picture for each word in your exercise book or your vocabulary notebook.

tower

staircase

Project

Portfolio

A famous castle

Find or draw a picture of a castle and write about it.

Bran Castle in Romania

A famous old castle is Bran Castle. It's in the centre of Romania. The castle is over seven hundred years old. The castle is on a ...

Your body

1 🔊 Read

Listen and read about the human body.

How your body changes during your life.

This baby is six months old. He can smile and sit but he can't walk yet.

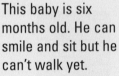

This little girl is two years old. She can walk, climb stairs and run, but she can't talk yet.

This child is seven years old. She can read, write, draw and count but she can't do Physics yet!

This woman is ninety years old. She can walk, but not very fast and she can't climb the stairs. She can read with glasses but she can't write or remember things very well.

This child is nine years old. He can ride a bike, he can swim and he can ski but he can't drive a car!

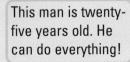

This man is twenty-five years old. He can do everything!

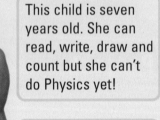

New words

- body • change • during • life • smile • yet
- climb • run • talk • draw • count • Physics
- ride a bike • ski • drive a car • everything
- fast • glasses • remember • things

2 Check

Complete the chart.

Age	Skill
6 months	_can smile and sit_
2 years	...
7 years	...
9 years	...
25 years	...
90 years	_can walk, but not very fast, can read with glasses_

3 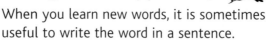 Listen

Listen and answer the questions.

1 How old is Sam's little sister, Susie?
2 What can she do?
3 What can't she do yet?

4 Speak

Tell the class.

- Have you got any younger brothers and sisters or cousins?
- How old are they?
- What things can they do?

> **Study tip**
>
> **Learning new words (3)**
>
> When you learn new words, it is sometimes useful to write the word in a sentence.
>
> _This young child can <u>ride</u> a bicycle._
>
> **Find three new words in the text and write a sentence for each word in your exercise book or vocabulary notebook.**

Project

Portfolio

What can they do?

Write about a family member or a friend. Say how old they are and what they can or can't do. Find a photograph or draw the person.

My sister
My little sister Charlotte
is only two years old but
she is very clever. She can
... and she can .... She can
also .... She says she can
..., too, but she can't!

Hurricanes and tornadoes

1 🔊 Read

Listen and read about hurricanes and tornadoes in the USA.

Welcome to www.wild-weather.com

Back Forward Stop Refresh Home AutoFill Print Mail

Address: @ http://www.wild-weather.com

www.Wild-Weather.com

In the USA a tornado or 'twister' can travel at 200km an hour.

Hurricane Mitch on the coast of Florida in 1998.

A hot sunny day in Florida

The USA is very big and the climate is different in different parts of the country. In the northern states for example, like Maine and Vermont, the weather is very cold in winter. It snows and you can ski. In the southern states, the climate is tropical. In Florida, the summer months (June, July and August) are very hot and sunny, but it often rains. It doesn't rain very much in winter and it's quite warm. Lots of people travel to Florida in December and January for the warm weather.

Hurricanes are violent storms.
They can move at 340 km an hour. On the east coast of the USA, the hurricane season is between May and November.

Tornadoes are also violent storms. They are called 'twisters' and can move at 200 km an hour. In the USA there are over a 1000 tornadoes every year. In the south of the USA the tornado season is from March to May. Tornadoes can lift houses into the air.

New words

- climate • different • part • northern • states • winter • southern
- tropical • summer • travel • hurricane • violent • storm • move
- coast • season • between • tornado • twister • every year
- lift • air

4 Speak

Talk to your partner.

- Is the climate the same in all parts of your country?
- What's the weather usually like in summer and winter?

2 Check

Right (✓) or wrong (✗)?

1 The weather is different in different states of the USA. ✓
2 Winters are very cold in Maine. ☐
3 Vermont has got a tropical climate. ☐
4 There are hurricanes on the east coast of the USA in May. ☐
5 There are tornados between May and November in the south of the USA. ☐

3  Listen

Listen and choose the correct weather for each scene.

① ② ③ ④

Study tip

Looking up words in a dictionary

When you use a dictionary to find the meaning of new words, it's much quicker if you know the alphabet well.

Write these words in alphabetical order as fast as you can.

- climate • different • every
- cold • from • for • big
- country • coast • enjoy
- February

Project

Portfolio

The climate in my country

Write a website article about the climate in your country. Draw weather maps for the summer and the winter and label them.

The climate in Spain
The climate in Spain is very nice. Summer is in June, July and August. It is usually very hot in summer. The temperature is usually...

Summer

Winter

Songs and raps

 Lesson 1, Exercise 7
The Greetings Rap

Listen.

Good morning, Toby!
Morning, Amy!
Hello, Tina!
Hi there, Mark!
She's my sister.
He's my brother.
Come here, Shep
And please don't bark!

 Lesson 2, Exercise 8
The Family Song

Listen and complete.

My brother and my [1]*sister*,
My mum and [2] ... and me,
We are the people
In my family.
My family, my family,
We are the people
In my family.

Say [3] ... to my brother,
[4] ... to sister Sue,
Good [5] ... to my mother
And to my father too.

Yes, my brother and my [6] ... ,
My mum and [7] ... and me,
We are the people
In my family.
My family, my family,
We are the people
In my family.

Say [8] ... to my brother,
[9] ... to sister Sue,
Say [10] ... to my mother
And to my father too.

 Lesson 3, Exercise 7
The Number Jive

Listen and complete.

[1]*One* and [2] ... and [3] ... , four, [4] ... .
Let's all do the Number Jive.
Six and [5] ... , eight, [6] ... , ten.
Let's go back and start again!

 Lesson 7, Exercise 7
The Mermaid Song

Listen and complete.

Sirena is a special girl.
She isn't like you or me.
Sirena is a mystery girl.
Where oh where is she?

Where oh where is Sirena?
Where oh where is [1] ... ?
Is she [2] ... the beach?
Is she [3] ... the tree?

Sirena is a special girl.
She isn't like you or me.
Sirena is a mermaid
And now she's [4] ... the sea.

Under the sea, under the sea,
She [5] ... happy, she is free.
But I miss you, Sirena.
Please come back to me.

 Lesson 8, Exercise 8
The Fruit Rap

Listen and complete.

An [1]*apple* or an [2] ... ,
A [3] ... or a [4] ... ,
These are OK
To eat on the beach.
I also like [5] ...
And all sorts of berries.
But my favourite fruit
Are juicy red [6] ...

 Lesson 13, Exercise 9

The Crazy House Song

Listen and complete.

In our crazy house,
In our crazy house,
There's a cat on the [1]*table*.
There's a shoe on the chair.
There's a plant on the [2] ...
And some grapes in my hair.
In our crazy house, yeah,
In our crazy house.

There's a goldfish in the [3] ... .
There are spiders on the floor.
There's a TV in the [4] ...
And there's one thing more.
In our crazy house, yeah,
In our crazy house.

There's a rock 'n' roll band,
Yes, a rock 'n' roll band.
There's a very loud noise
Wham Bam! Wham Bam!
There's a rock 'n' roll band,
Yes a rock 'n' roll band
In the [5] ... !

92

Lesson 17, Exercise 9

The Funny Farm Rap

Listen.

I've got an uncle.
His name is Uncle Jack.
He's got a farm
In the Australian outback.
There aren't any sheep
On Uncle Jack's farm,
And there aren't any wolves
To do any harm.
But there are some animals
You only see in zoos.
Eighty-six crocodiles
And ninety kangaroos!

Lesson 18, Exercise 10

The Time Song

Listen and complete.

It's ten to nine on ¹*Monday*
And I am late for school.
I'm late again on ² ... ,
It really isn't cool.
But I'm not late on ³ ... ,
And when it's ⁴ ... ,
I'm really very happy
Because on ⁵ ... we're free! We're free!
On ⁶ ... we're free!

Lesson 23, Exercise 6

The Body Rap

Listen and complete.

Touch your ¹*eye*, nose, mouth and ² ... ,
Then your ³ ... . Now go from here.
⁴ A... and ⁵ h... , finger and ⁶ t... ,
Back and shoulder, one by one,
Leg and ⁷ k... , foot and ⁸ t... ,
Clap your hands and off you go!

Lesson 26, Exercise 8

The Clothes Song

Listen and complete.

My ¹*trousers* don't fit
And my ² ... is split,
And I'm going out tonight
I've got nothing to wear,
Only a pair
Of ³ ... , and they're too tight!

My ⁴ ... 's too long
And my ⁵ ... 's wrong,
And I'm going out tonight,
I've got nothing to wear,
Only a pair
Of ⁶ ... , and they're too tight!

My ⁷ ... are worn
And my ⁸ ... is torn,
And I'm going out tonight,
I've got nothing to wear,
Only a pair
Of ⁹ ... , and they're too tight!
My boots – they're just too tight!

Lesson 28, Exercise 8
Vicky the Vampire Song

Listen and complete.

I ¹*go* to bed in the morning.
I ² ... all through the day.
I ³ ... late in the evening.
That's when I like to play.

Yes, I am Vicky the Vampire!
Vampires sleep all day!
I am Vicky the Vampire!
Vampires rule, OK!

She ⁴ ... to bed in the morning.
She ⁵ ... all through the day.
She ⁶ ... late in the evening.
That's when she likes to play.

Yes, she is Vicky the Vampire!
Vampires sleep all day!
She is Vicky the Vampire!
Vampires rule, OK!

Lesson 33, Exercise 9
The Weather Rap

Listen and complete.

The weather's ¹*cold*,
And very ² ... .
The temperature is minus three.
Look, it's ³ ... !
Now it's ⁴ ... !
Let's go home and have some tea.

Now it's ⁵ ... .
The sun is ⁶ ... .
It's a really brilliant day.
It's warm and ⁷ ... ,
And I'm happy,
Because I'm now on holiday!

Lesson 36, Exercise 6
The Job Song

Listen and complete.

I'm a ¹*chef* in a restaurant.
I work there every day.
I cook the food and ² ... the bread.
That's how I earn my pay.

I'm a ³ ... in a school.
I work there every day.
I ⁴ ... young children how to read.
That's how I earn my pay.

I'm a ⁵ ... in a garage.
I work there every day.
I ⁶ ... big cars for millionaires.
That's how I earn my pay.

We work hard every day!
That's how we earn our pay!

Lesson 38, Exercise 4
The Map Rap

It's next to the supermarket,
Opposite the park,
In front of the station,
Near the car park.
It's next to a café
And the bus stop.
My Kind of Music
Is my favourite shop.

94

Banjo's useful lists

Lesson 3, Exercise 2
Numbers 1–50

Listen and repeat the numbers.

1 one   2 two   3 three   4 four   5 five   6 six
7 seven   8 eight   9 nine   10 ten   11 eleven
12 twelve   13 thirteen   14 fourteen   15 fifteen
16 sixteen   17 seventeen 18 eighteen
19 nineteen   20 twenty   21 twenty-one
30 thirty   31 thirty-one
40 forty   41 forty-one   50 fifty

Lesson 8, Exercise 5
Colours

Listen and repeat the colours.

- yellow • red • green • orange • pink • brown
- purple • turquoise • beige • grey • black
- white • blue • dark blue • light blue

Lesson 17, Exercise 5
Numbers 50–100

Listen and repeat the numbers.

Lesson 18, Exercise 6
Days of the week

Listen and repeat the days of the week.

Monday   Tuesday   Wednesday   Thursday   Friday
Saturday   Sunday
Saturday and Sunday = the weekend

Lesson 22, Exercise 5
British money

Listen and repeat the British money.

£20 = twenty pounds
£10 = ten pounds
£5 = five pounds
£1 = one pound/a pound
£2.50 = two pounds fifty (pence)/two fifty
£1.50 = one pound fifty (pence)/one fifty
50p = fifty p/fifty pence

Lesson 37, Exercise 3
Ordinal numbers

Listen and repeat the ordinal numbers.

1st first   2nd second   3rd third   4th fourth
5th fifth   6th sixth   7th seventh   8th eighth
9th ninth   10th tenth   11th eleventh
12th twelfth   13th thirteenth   14th fourteenth
15th fifteenth   16th sixteenth   17th seventeenth
18th eighteenth   19th nineteenth
20th twentieth   21st twenty-first
30th thirtieth   31st thirty-first

Note
You write: May 1st but you say: May the first

Banjo's Grammar Store

Welcome to Banjo's Grammar Store! Open the doors and choose!

1 Verb: *to be*	13 Verb: *have got*
2 Personal pronouns	14 Verb: *can* (ability)
3 Possessive adjectives	15 Verb: *can* (requests)
4 Object pronouns	16 Imperative form
5 Indefinite article: *a/an*	17 Present simple tense
6 Definite article: *the*	18 Adverbs of frequency
7 Demonstrative pronouns	19 Present continuous tense
8 Pronouns: *some* and *any*	20 Present simple and present continuous
9 Possessive *'s*	21 Verb: *want* + infinitive with *to*
10 Noun plurals	22 Verb: *let's* + infinitive without *to*
11 Question words	
12 Prepositions	

① Verb *to be* singular

Positive

Long		Short
I am Toby.	=	I'm Toby.
You are Amy.	=	You're Amy.
He is Mark.	=	He's Mark.
She is Tina.	=	She's Tina.
It is Shep.	=	It's Shep.

Negative

Long		Short
I am not your teacher.	=	I'm not your teacher.
You are not my student.	=	You aren't my student.
He is not my brother.	=	He isn't my brother.
She is not my sister.	=	She isn't my sister.
It is not a dog.	=	It isn't a dog.

Yes/No questions

Are you Mark?	Yes, I am./No, I'm not.
Is he a teacher?	Yes, he is./No, he isn't.

Verb *to be* plural.

Positive

Long		Short
We are brothers.	=	We're brothers.
You are sisters.	=	You're sisters.
They are friends.	=	They're friends.

Negative

Long		Short
We are not brothers.	=	We aren't brothers.
You are not sisters.	=	You aren't sisters.
They are not friends.	=	They aren't friends.

Yes/No questions

Are you sisters?	Yes, we are./No, we aren't.
Are they friends?	Yes, they are./No, they aren't.

② Personal pronouns

I	**I**'m Toby.
you	**You**'re Amy.
he	**He**'s Mark.
she	**She**'s Tina.
it	**It**'s Shep.
we	**We**'re Amy and Toby.
you	**You**'re Mark and Tina.
they	**They**'re Kelly and Jack.

③ Possessive adjectives

my	**My** name is Toby.
your	**Your** name is Amy.
his	**His** name is Mark.
her	**Her** name is Tina.
its	**Its** name is Shep.
our	**Our** names are Amy and Toby.
your	**Your** names are Mark and Tina.
their	**Their** names are Kelly and Jack.

④ Object pronouns

me	He likes **me**.
you	I like **you**.
him	I like **him**.
her	I like **her**.
it	I like **it**.
us	They like **us**.
you	I like **you**.
them	I like **them**.

⑤ Indefinite article: *a/an*

It's **a** table.
It's **an** apple.

⑥ Definite article: *the*

Where's **the** apple?   It's on **the** table.
He's in **the** garden.

⑦ Demonstrative pronouns: *this*, *that*, *these* and *those*

 **This** is my mother.

 What's **that**? It's a book.

 **These** are my friends.

 What are **those**? They're pineapples.

⑧ Pronouns: *some* and *any*

Positive		Negative	
There is	**a** poster.	There isn't	**a** poster.
There is	**an** apple.	There isn't	**an** apple.
There are	**some** plants.	There aren't	**any** plants.

Yes/No questions

Is there **a** poster?	Yes, there is. / No, there isn't.
Is there **an** apple?	Yes, there is. / No, there isn't.
Any there **any** plants?	Yes, there are. / No, there aren't.

⑨ Possessive 's

singular		plural
This is	Toby**'s** camera.	my parent**s'** car
	Amy**'s** watch.	the teacher**s'** room

⑩ Noun plurals

one chair	two chair**s**
one grape	three grape**s**
one mango	four mango**es**
one peach	five peach**es**
one country	six countr**ies**

⑪ Question words

What	**What**'s this?	It's a mobile phone.
	What colour is it?	It's pink and red.
	What time is it?	It's four o'clock.
Who	**Who**'s she?	She's my sister.
How old	**How old** are you?	I'm eleven.
Where	**Where** are you from?	I'm from Spain.
	Where's Amy?	She's in the bathroom.
When	**When**'s the film?	It's on Tuesday at six o'clock.
Why	**Why** are you tired?	Because it's late.
How much	**How much** is it?	It's £1.50.
How many	**How many** people are there?	There are five.

⑫ Prepositions

in	Mark's **in** the bathroom.	from	He's **from** Italy.
	Rome is **in** Italy.	to	I go **to** the park every Friday.
on	The dog is **on** the sofa.		Can you count from one **to** fifty?
	My birthday's **on** June 14th.	at	He's **at** school.
under	The book is **under** the desk.		The film is **at** five o'clock.
behind	The cat is **behind** the chair.	of	Madrid is the capital **of** Spain.
in front of	The bus stop is **in front of** the school.	with	I like coffee **with** milk.
next to	The cinema is **next to** the supermarket.	for	I have sandwiches **for** lunch.
opposite	The park is **opposite** the swimming pool.		

⑬ Verb: *have got*

Positive

I've got red and blue hair.

Long	*Short*
I have got brown hair.	= I've got brown hair.
You have got blue eyes.	= You've got blue eyes.
He has got spiky hair.	= He's got spiky hair.
She has got wavy hair.	= She's got wavy hair.
It has got a tail.	= It's got a tail.
We have got a car.	= We've got a car.
You have got some ponies.	= You've got some ponies.
They have got some chickens.	= They've got some chickens.

Negative

Long	*Short*
I have not got black hair.	= I haven't got black hair.
You have not got green eyes.	= You haven't got green eyes.
He has not got curly hair.	= He hasn't got curly hair.
She has not got grey hair.	= She hasn't got grey hair.
It has not got a long neck.	= It hasn't got a long neck.
We have not got any goats.	= We haven't got any goats.
You have not got any ducks.	= You haven't got any ducks.
They have not got any sheep.	= They haven't got any sheep.

Yes/No questions

Have you got brown eyes?	Yes, I have. / No, I haven't.
Has she got long hair?	Yes, she has. / No, she hasn't.

⑭ Verb: *can* (ability)

Positive

I can sing.
You can use a computer.
He can ride a horse.
She can play the piano.
It can swim.
We can sail a boat.
You can read a map.
They can play table tennis.

Negative

Long	*Short*
I cannot sing.	= I can't sing.
You cannot use a computer.	= You can't use a computer.
He cannot ride a horse.	= He can't ride a horse.
She cannot play the piano.	= She can't play the piano.
It cannot swim.	= It can't swim.
We cannot sail a boat.	= We can't sail a boat.
You cannot read a map.	= You can't read a map.
They cannot play table tennis.	= They can't play table tennis.

Yes/No questions

Can you use a computer?	Yes, I can. / No, I can't.
Can he ride a horse?	Yes, he can. / No, he can't.

(15) Verb: *can* (requests)

Can I have an ice cream, please?
Can I have a banana milkshake, please?

(16) Verb: imperative form

Positive	Negative
Come here!	**Don't** come here!
Sit down!	**Don't** sit down!

(17) Present simple tense

Positive	Negative	Yes/No questions
I like those jeans.	I don't like that T-shirt.	Do you like eggs?
You like tigers.	You don't like chimpanzees.	Yes, I do./No, I don't.
He likes Britney Spears.	He doesn't like Robbie Williams.	Does he like the trousers?
She likes computer games.	She doesn't like football.	Yes, he does./No, he doesn't.
It likes plants and fruit.	It doesn't like meat.	
We like trainers.	We don't like boots.	
You like giraffes.	You don't like elephants.	
They like videos.	They don't like homework.	

(18) Adverbs of frequency

I **always** do my homework.
He **usually** plays football after school.
She **often** watches a video on Saturday.
We **sometimes** play cards.
They **never** walk home from school.

I am **always** happy.
He is **usually** happy.
She is **often** hungry.
We are **sometimes** bored in class.
They are **never** late for school.

(19) Present continuous tense

Positive

Long		Short
I am doing my homework.	=	I'm doing my homework.
You are watching a video.	=	You're watching a video.
He is playing football.	=	He's playing football.
She is reading a book.	=	She's reading a book.
It is walking.	=	It's walking.
We are listening to the radio.	=	We're listening to the radio.
You are shopping.	=	You're shopping.
They are making a cake.	=	They're making a cake.

Negative

Long		Short	Yes/No Questions
I am not walking home.	=	I'm not walking home.	Are you wearing sunglasses?
You are not making a sandwich.	=	You're not making a sandwich.	Yes, I am./No, I'm not.
He is not swimming.	=	He isn't swimming.	Is he doing his homework?
She is not taking a photo.	=	She isn't taking a photo.	Yes, he is./No, he isn't.
It is not raining.	=	It isn't raining.	
We are not washing the car.	=	We aren't washing the car.	
You are not staying in a hotel.	=	You aren't staying in a hotel.	
They are sending an email.	=	They aren't sending an email.	

20 Present simple and present continuous

I work in a garage.
In this picture I'm repairing a car.

I work in a restaurant.
In this picture I'm serving a customer.

21 Verb: *want* + infinitive with *to*

Positive

I want to buy a CD.
You want to have lunch.
He wants to play computer games.
She wants to go to the cinema.
It wants to eat.
We want to stay in a hotel.
You want to watch television.
They want to take a photo.

Negative

I don't want to buy a CD.
You don't want to have lunch.
He doesn't want to play computer games.
She doesn't want to go to the cinema.
It doesn't want to eat.
We don't want to stay in a hotel.
You don't want to watch television.
They don't want to take a photo.

Yes/No Questions

Do you want to have lunch?
Does he want to play computer games?

Yes, I do./No, I don't.
Yes, he does./No, he doesn't.

22 Verb: *let's* + infinitive without *to*

Let's   go to the cinema.
             have a party.
             see a film.
             play some computer games.

Let's have a party!

Word list

Lesson 1
Titles
Miss
Mr
Mrs
_____
Greetings
Good afternoon.
Good evening.
Good morning.
_____
am
brother
he
Hello!
Hi!
I
is
my
name
she
sister
Thank you.
Welcome to
   [Bristol].
what
who

Lesson 2
Family
aunt
brother
cousin
daughter
father (dad)
grandfather
grandmother
husband
mother (mum)
parents
sister
son
uncle
wife
_____
and
are
cat
clever
dog
family
friendly
her
his
little
me
our
pretty
this
very
you

Lesson 3
Numbers 1–50
one
two
three
four
five
six
seven
eight
nine
ten
eleven
twelve
thirteen
fourteen
fifteen
sixteen
seventeen
eighteen
nineteen
twenty
twenty-one
thirty
thirty-one
forty
forty-one
fifty
_____
Bye.
class
Goodbye.
Here's [Miss
   Kent].
How old are
   you?
Me too.
No, I'm not.
OK.
See you later.
Ssh!
teacher
too
Year [7]
Yes, I am.
Yes./No.

Lesson 4
boy
cottage
here
hungry
in
isn't
strange
the
This way!
tomorrow
where
woods

Lesson 5
bag
correct
find
match
match (n)
Miss one turn.
most
must
partner
person
Pick a number.
point (n)
put back
say
score
sentence
square
Take turns.
then
used
winner

Lesson 6
**Countries and
   nationalities**
Argentina –
   Argentinian
Brazil – Brazilian
China – Chinese
France – French
Germany –
   German
Greece – Greek
Italy – Italian
Poland – Polish
Portugal –
   Portuguese
Russia – Russian
Spain – Spanish
Turkey – Turkish
the UK (Great
   Britain) – British
the USA
   (America) –
   American
_____
a/an
at
best friend
but
English
from
guys
in [Italian]
interesting
love
nice
number
PS

Rome
school
surname
they're
we're

Lesson 7
**Prepositions of
   place**
behind
in
on
under
_____
a
apple
bad
book
box
Catch!
chair
desk
egg
good
ice cream
it
Look!
mobile phone
now
orange (n)
silly
table
that
That's right.
this
trick
Yuk!

Lesson 8
Fruit
banana(s)
cherry(-ies)
grape(s)
lemon(s)
lime(s)
mango(es)
melon(s)
peach(es)
pear(s)
pineapple(s)
plum(s)
strawberry(-ies)

Colours
beige
black
blue
brown
dark blue
green
grey

light blue
orange (adj)
pink
purple
red
turquoise
white
yellow
_____
all over the world
best
buy
the Caribbean
colour
Come to …
Excuse me.
fruit
funny
Have a [taste].
I don't know.
market
Ooh!
sour
South America
sweet
thanks
these
those
town

Lesson 9
age
Australia(n)
beautiful
big
Canada(-ian)
capital
capital letter
city
country
east
England
favourite
first name
home town
India
Lyon
nationality
north
photo
pronoun
school trip
south

Lesson 10
Irish
Manchester
Oh!

Lesson 11
The house
bathroom
bedroom
dining room
garage
garden
hall
kitchen
sitting room
stairs
toilet
_____
car
Come in.
Cool!
friends
house
of
palace
their
Wow!

Lesson 12
**Common
   possessions**
camera
computer
computer game
cricket bat
Discman
radio
skateboard
stereo
_____
against
all right
ball
bike
[I'm] bored.
bowl (v)
CD
Come on.
cricket
game
girl
[It's] fun.
Never mind.
Oh no!
team
watch (n)
What about [a
   game of
   cricket]?
window
with
You're wrong.

Lesson 13
House and furniture
armchair
bed
cupboard
door
lamp
plant
poster
sofa
television/TV
wardrobe

also
any
deck
flat
for
great
home
houseboat
live
river
some
student
summer
there

Lesson 14
band
competition
final
hotel
junior
listen
Los Angeles
pop star
ready
records
small
song
star
winner

Lesson 15
answer
sorry
thing

Lesson 16
Hair styles and colours
blonde
curly
fair
long
medium length
short
spiky
straight
wavy

autograph
Best wishes
dear
eyes
film star
got

hair
I know.
old
or
Please write soon.
really
tall

Lesson 17
Animals
calf(-ves)
chick(s)
chicken(s)
cow(s)
duck(s)
goat(s)
goose (geese)
horse(s)
lamb(s)
pony(-ies)
sheep

Numbers 50–100
fifty
fifty-one
sixty
sixty-one
seventy
seventy-one
eight
eighty-one
ninety
ninety-one
a hundred

about (adv)
Come and look.
Cornwall
different
dinosaur(s)
Don't be silly!
everyone
farm
It's only a joke.
ostriches
so
sort of
south-west
town house

Lesson 18
The time
It's one o'clock.
five past
ten past
quarter past
twenty past
twenty-five past
half past
twenty-five to
twenty to
quarter to
ten to
five to

Days of the week
Monday
Tuesday
Wednesday
Thursday
Friday
Saturday
Sunday

about (prep)
at [four o'clock]
C U (see you)
cinema
day
Er ...
film
hopeless
How R U? (How are you?)
Hurry up!
insects
late
lecture
new
next
No, thanks.
on [TV]
tiger(s)
today
TV programme
Warsaw
week
What's the time?
What time is it?
Why?
wild

Lesson 19
Houses
apartment
block of flats
cottage
detached house
terraced house

apple tree
balcony
Belfast
comma
downstairs
full stop
join
list
lots of
more than
near
neighbours
noisy
own
park
pet
quiet
quite
road
sometimes
start
street
swimming pool
upstairs

Lesson 21
24 hours
adventure camp
can/can't/ cannot
child (children)
do
exciting
food
have fun
horrible
learn
not very well
telephone
thing(s)
well (conj)

Free time
make an omelette
play chess
play table tennis
play the guitar
play the piano
read a map
ride a horse
sail a boat
sing a song
skateboard (v)
swim under water
use a computer

Lesson 22
Food and drink
cola
hot chocolate
lemonade
milkshake(s)
mineral water
orange juice

banana (adj)
Can I help you?
chocolate (adj)
count
drink (n)
flavour(s)
How much is/are ... ?
only
pence/p
pound
strawberry (adj)
sure
vanilla (adj)
Yes, please.

Lesson 23
The body
arm
back
ear
eye
finger
foot (feet)
hand
head
knee
leg

mouth
neck
nose
shoulder
stomach
thumb
toe
tooth (teeth)

Verbs
close
draw
hold up
jump
open
point
put
sit down
stand up
touch

boyfriend
cold
don't
down
goal
Hey!
over there
pockets
rude
see
up
watch (v)
you two

Lesson 24
boring
cave
dive
Egypt
far
holiday
man (men)
over here
queen
speak English
statue
surprise
Venice
wait
weekend
woman (women)

Lesson 25
finish
follow
in pairs
instructions
land
play
throw

Lesson 26
Clothes
baseball cap
boots
dress
jeans
jumper

shoes
skirt
socks
top
trainers
trousers
T-shirt

Adjectives
brilliant
cool
great
horrible
ugly
wicked

Pronouns
me
you
him
her
it
us
you
them

a lot
clothes
go away
gold
Here you are.
Huh!
Leave us alone.
Mmm.
not very much
sequins
silver
single
Uh, uh!
What about you?

Lesson 27
Verbs
climb
eat
hunt
live
run
sleep
swing
walk

Africa
Asia
because
chimpanzee
elephant
fast
giraffe
like
jungle
meat
night
rain forest
tiger
tree
visit
wildlife park

Lesson 28
Daily routines
do homework
finish school
get up
go to bed
go to school
have breakfast
have dinner
have lunch
play computer
  games
play sport
start school
watch TV

actor
all
bass guitar
called
card trick
cereal
cup
diet
early
hate
not much
punk
says
school holidays
toast
together

Lesson 29
School subjects
Art
Domestic Science
Drama
English
French
Games
Geography
History
I.C.T.
  (Information
  and
  Communication
  Technology)
Maths
  (Mathematics)
P.E. (Physical
  Education)
R.E. (Religious
  Education)
Science
Spanish

again
basketball
before
cafeteria
club
elementary
  school
grade
in the afternoon
in the morning
language
lesson

secondary school
study period
subject
then

Lesson 30
opposite (n)
mad

Lesson 31
**Everyday
  activities**
go to bed
go to sleep
have a snack
listen to music
meet friends
play cards
play football
read in bed
walk home
watch a video

**Adverbs of
  frequency**
always
never
often
sometimes
usually

everybody
good at
in bed
late for
later
next door
page

Lesson 32
**Everyday
  activities**
do my homework
have a shower
listen to the
  radio
make a sandwich
take a photo
talk to a friend
wash the car
write a story
write an email

don't be daft
drop
project
sit

Lesson 33
Weather
It's cloudy.
It's cold.
It's foggy.
It's hot.
It's raining.
It's snowing.
It's sunny. / The
  sun is shining.
It's warm.
It's windy.

at the moment
café
like (prep)
mom
next to
shop (v)
stay
sunglasses
swim (v)
swimming pool
wear
weather

Lesson 34
at work
coat
department
detective
job
leave
lift
lovely
outside
people
store
train
Well done!

Lesson 35
picture

Lesson 36
Work
bus driver
chef
cook
dentist
doctor
garage
hospital
look after
mechanic
nurse
office
repair
restaurant
school
secretary
serve
shop assistant
supermarket
teach
teacher
type
waiter
work

baby
customer
every day
hold
make
pizza
sports car

Lesson 37
**Months of
  the year**
January
February
March
April
May
June
July
August
September
October
November
December

Ordinal numbers
1st–31st

Bad luck!
birthday
Christmas
date
get
guess
month
present(s)
year

Lesson 38
Places in town
book shop
bus stop
café
car park
cinema
computer shop
newsagent
pet shop
record shop
station
supermarket
swimming pool

**Prepositions
  of place**
in front of
next to
opposite

busy
good idea
Let's … .
magazine
over there
party
planetarium
want to
Where's [the
  computer
  shop]?

Lesson 39
**Festivals and
  special days**
Christmas Day
Christmas Eve
Easter
Easter Sunday
Halloween
Thanksgiving

dark
decorations
famous
fancy dress
festival
fortune
give thanks
hide
hot cross buns
lamb
lights
look for
meal
money
play a trick
pudding
pumpkin pie
remember
settlers
stockings
sweet potatoes
sweets
traditional
treat
turkey

Lesson 40
motorbike

**Across the
  curriculum 1**
**English-speaking
  countries**
Australia
Canada
New Zealand
South Africa
the Republic of
  Ireland
the UK
the USA

bus
hamburger
main
million
taxi
tennis
walkman

**Across the
  curriculum 2**
bottom
castle
centre
chapel
mountains
over
rock
Romania
sea
square (adj)
staircase
store rooms
top
tourist
tower
view
Wales
wall

**Across the
  curriculum 3**
body
change
drive a car
during
everything
glasses
life
Physics
ride a bike
ski
smile
talk
yet

**Across the
  curriculum 4**
air
between
climate
coast
dictionary
hurricane
if
km an hour
lift (v)
like
meaning
move
northern
part
quicker
season
southern
states
storm
tornado
travel
tropical
twister
use
violent
winter